"The poems in *The Treasure of His Company* are poignant, amusing, and touching. The stories lead us to contemplate the heart of God, who is our peace and dwelling place."

*Mrs. Mary Turner, Haliburton, Ontario, Canada*

"In this book, *The Treasure of His Company*, there are tears, heartfelt hardships, memories, courage, trust in God, faith, hope, love, mountaintops and valley experiences. I believe this book was written by the finger of God, in guidance to Jan."

*Mrs. Roberta Hooper, Orillia, Ontario, Canada*

"In *The Treasure of His Company,* Jan has written a beautiful book of devotions, illustrated with her drawings as well as quotations from the Bible and Christian writers. A treasure!"

*Mrs. Doreen Marley, Orillia, Ontario, Canada*

# The Treasure of His Company

A Collection of Devotional Poetry
& Meditations Vol. 1.
Jan Howlett

"For where your treasure is,
there will your heart be also."

Matthew 6:21

For you are precious to God

*Jan Howlett*
*Ps. 16:11*
*2005*

# The Treasure of His Company

Essence
PUBLISHING

Belleville, Ontario, Canada

# The Treasure of His Company

Presented To: _____

Date: _____

# The Treasure of His Company:

## A Collection of Devotional Poetry & Meditations Vol. 1

### Written & Illustrated By
### Jan Howlett

John 21:15

Printed in Canada
by
*Essence* PUBLISHING

# The Treasure of His Company:
## A Collection of Devotional Poetry & Meditations Vol. 1

Original Watercolour Paintings, Interior Artwork,
and
Cover: "Royal Monarch"
By: Jan Howlett
Copyright 2005

© 1988-1999 Corel Corp. Corel Draw 9 Credit: 9 Clipart Graphics Suite

*All Rights Reserved. No part of this publication may be reproduced, stored in a retrieval system or transmitted in any form or by any means—electronic, mechanical, photocopy, recording or any other—except for brief quotations in printed reviews, without the prior permission of the author.*

All Scripture quotations, unless otherwise specified, are from *The Holy Bible, King James Version.* The World Publishing Company, Cleveland & N.Y. Scriptures marked NIV are from *The Holy Bible, New International Version.* Copyright © 1973, 1978, 1984 International Bible Society. Used by permission of Zondervan Publishing House. All rights reserved. Scripture quotations marked AMP are taken from *The Amplified Bible*, Old Testament copyright © 1965, 1987 by the Zondervan Corporation. *The Amplified New Testament*, copyright © 1954, 1958, 1987 by the Lockman Foundation. Used by permission. Scripture quotations marked NASB are taken from the *New American Standard Bible*, copyright © The Lockman Foundation 1960, 1962, 1963, 1968, 1971, 1972, 1973, 1977. All rights reserved.

### E-Mail: hislambs@csolve.net

**Library and Archives Canada Cataloguing in Publication**

Howlett, Jan, 1946-
 The treasure of his company : a collection of devotional poetry & meditations / written & illustrated by Jan Howlett.

ISBN 1-55306-882-3 (v. 1)

 1. Christian poetry, Canadian (English). 2. Meditations. I. Title.

PS8615.O948T74 2004     C811'.6     C2004-907128-9

Dedicated

# To The Glory Of God

And

To Ross, my precious husband,
who has assisted me with so many facets
of this work.
His godly example and
consistent walk with the Lord
encourages me daily to be faithful,
to write obediently to the Lord's desire alone
and to always keep
Christ and His Word
the central message in all that I do,
whether with my pen or with my paintbrush.

# Table of Contents

*Acknowledgements* . . . . . . . . . . . . . . . . . . . . . . . . . . . .17
*Foreword* . . . . . . . . . . . . . . . . . . . . . . . . . . . . . . . . . . .21
*Preface* . . . . . . . . . . . . . . . . . . . . . . . . . . . . . . . . . . . . .23
*Introduction* . . . . . . . . . . . . . . . . . . . . . . . . . . . . . . . .25
Treasured Invitation . . . . . . . . . . . . . . . . . . . . . . . . . .30
From Such Treasures, Flee! . . . . . . . . . . . . . . . . . . . .32
The Secret Place of Heart's Content!/Meditation . . . . . . . .33
A Lamp And A Light . . . . . . . . . . . . . . . . . . . . . . . . .37
Scripture Text: Psalm 91 . . . . . . . . . . . . . . . . . . . . . .41
Yield To His Grasp . . . . . . . . . . . . . . . . . . . . . . . . . .43
By Special Request! . . . . . . . . . . . . . . . . . . . . . . . . . .44
God's Salvation Gift! . . . . . . . . . . . . . . . . . . . . . . . . .48
No Small Thing? . . . . . . . . . . . . . . . . . . . . . . . . . . . .50
Washed In The Blood of The Lamb/Meditation . . . . . . . . .54
Honour And Remembrance/Meditation . . . . . . . . . . . . . .58
Honour And Remembrance . . . . . . . . . . . . . . . . . . . .60
God's Precious Remembrance Book! . . . . . . . . . . . . .62
God's Mercies Bring Joy . . . . . . . . . . . . . . . . . . . . . .65
The Old Road Home . . . . . . . . . . . . . . . . . . . . . . . . .66
Trusting The Arm of God/Meditation . . . . . . . . . . . . . . . .68
But Lord, Who Am I? . . . . . . . . . . . . . . . . . . . . . . . .71
Hannah's Desire . . . . . . . . . . . . . . . . . . . . . . . . . . . .76
Ministering Life . . . . . . . . . . . . . . . . . . . . . . . . . . . . .79
Lessons Simply Painted, Not Spoken! . . . . . . . . . . . .82
Silent Sufferings . . . . . . . . . . . . . . . . . . . . . . . . . . . .84
Patience And Desert Honey!/Meditation . . . . . . . . . . . . . .87
Patience And Desert Honey! . . . . . . . . . . . . . . . . . . .88
Safe Ice?/Meditation . . . . . . . . . . . . . . . . . . . . . . . . . . . .91
Safe Ice? . . . . . . . . . . . . . . . . . . . . . . . . . . . . . . . . . .92
Proving Grounds/Meditation . . . . . . . . . . . . . . . . . . . . .106

| | |
|---|---|
| Proving Grounds | 108 |
| Loved By One Who Loves God! | 112 |
| Love's Treasure | 114 |
| Birthday Cards Sent From God!/Meditation | 120 |
| Birthday Cards Sent From God! | 122 |
| Alone, But God! | 125 |
| Bent But Not Broken | 127 |
| Ambush, Earthquakes and Blooming In The Dark! | 128 |
| Jesus Knows Every Teardrop | 130 |
| No More Mud Please!/Meditation | 131 |
| Under His Tender Watch Care/Meditation | 136 |
| A Wall With No Door! | 140 |
| Silks Of Ease | 142 |
| Shipwreck: Fickle Soft South Winds | 148 |
| Songbirds, Not Fighter Jets!/Meditation | 151 |
| Sweet Little Willy! | 153 |
| Exactly What I Need/Meditation | 158 |
| Precious Heavenly Father/A Prayer | 161 |
| Eager For His Return?/Meditation | 164 |
| Jesus Is the Treasure! | 169 |
| The Treasure of His Company | 170 |
| Angels With Coloured Strings Attached!/Meditation | 171 |
| Where Your Treasure Is/Meditation | 176 |
| My Rock and My Salvation/Music | 179 |
| Devotional Notes | 182 |
| Folio Art Notes | 192 |
| Bibliography | 196 |
| FHLM General Background History, Ministry Purpose & Information | 198 |
| Product Order Forms | 203 |

# Table of Contents: Illustrations

Photographs, Sketches, Watercolours (WC)

Butterfly/WC Vignettes . . . . . . . . . . . .27, 128, 175, 182, 183
Butterfly Chrysalis/WC . . . . . . . . . . . . . . . . . . . . . . . .128
Twin Hearts/Clipart . . . . . . . . . . . . . . . . . . . . . . . . . .24
Hands Of Invitation: Engagement Ring/Sketch . . . . . . . . . . 26
Mikado Train Engine/"Glorious Journey"/WC/
      & Inset/Folio . . . . . . . . . . . . . . . . .28, 29, F-97
White N.A. Butterfly/"Winged Treasures"/WC/
      Folio . . . . . . . . . . . . . . . . . . . . . . .31, F-102
Map of Newfoundland/Sketch . . . . . . . . . . . . . . . . . . . . .36
Twin Lambs/Photo . . . . . . . . . . . . . . . . . . . . . . . . . . .42
11:59 & Counting! Don't Delay/Sketch . . . . . . . . . . . . . . .47
Open Bible/Photo . . . . . . . . . . . . . . . . . . . . . . .48, 125
Royal Geranium/J's Photos . . . . . . . . . . . . . . . . . . . . .53
Three Crosses/Clipart . . . . . . . . . . . . . . . . . . . . . . . . .57
Purple Finch/J's Photos . . . . . . . . . . . . . . . . . . . . . . . .60
Anniversary Red Rose Vignette/J's Photos/Folio . . . . . . .62, F-104
Guthrie: "The Old Road Home"/WC/Folio . . . . . . .65, F-103
Hannah's Vase/Sketch . . . . . . . . . . . . . . . . . . . . . . . .75, 76
Beaverton Estate/"Favourite Forest"/
      WC/& Inset/Folio . . . . . . . . . .80, 81, 82, F-103
Apples/WC/Folio . . . . . . . . . . . . . . . . . . . . . . . . .86, F-104
Blue Desert Poppy/WC . . . . . . . . . . . . . . . . . . . . . . . .88
Ice Pond/J's Photos . . . . . . . . . . . . . . . . . . . . . . . . . .90
Colour Centre Folio–15 Graphics Collection . . . . . . . . .97–104

Horse—Lacy's First Prize—Country Fair/
J's Photos/Folio . . . . . . . . . . . . .F-100, 105
Doreen's Amaryllis: Under Lenses/J's Photos/Folio . . .F-101, 108
Jan's Cameo/Sketch . . . . . . . . . . . . . . . . . . . . . . . . . . . . .111
Chickadees/Sketch . . . . . . . . . . . . . . . . . . . . . . . . . .114, 115
Jerusalem Lilies/"Glorious Resurrection"/WC
& Inset/Folio . . . . . .F-101, 118, 119, 121
Cameo Grey Rose Bud/J's Photos . . . . . . . . . . . . . . . . . . .123
Gyrfalcon/"Invitation To Worship"/WC/Folio . . . . .F-99, 135
Old Oak Tree-Avocet/"God's Strength"/WC . . . . . . . . . .138
Wall With No Door/WC . . . . . . . . . . . . . . . . . . . . . . . . . .140
Silks Throne/WC . . . . . . . . . . . . . . . . . . . . . . . . . . . . . . . .141
Shipwreck/Sketch . . . . . . . . . . . . . . . . . . . . . . . . . . . . . . .147
Little Willy on my lap:/J's Photos/Folio . . . . . . . . . .F-98, 150
Gannets: "Commitment"/WC/Folio . . . . . . . . . . . . .F-98, 157
White Doves/"God's Love"/WC/&Inset/
Folio . . . . . . . . . . . . . . . .F-100, 162, 163
Little Friends/"Friends Forever"/WC . . . . . . . . . . . . . . . .166
Snow Fence/"God's Cleansing Power"/WC/Folio . . .F-102, 169
Little Willy Waiting Patiently/J's Photos . . . . . . . . . . . . .178
Hands Of Invitation with Wedding Ring/Sketch/Hearts . . . .24, 181
Flying Fish/WC/Folio . . . . . . . . . . . . . . . . . . . . .F-97, Various

# Acknowledgements

Usually a worthwhile project reaches completion because many have worked diligently together as a team, though behind the scenes they are often unseen and unsung. Nevertheless, those same workers share in the final presentation. Those who have assisted me in this endeavour of love are many. Some are heroes of history past. Others are loved ones; either living or with the Lord in Glory.

As I look back today, I am grateful to the Lord for allowing me to struggle through my high school English Composition classes. It was in those classes that the desire to write a book someday began to germinate.

I am also thankful for a special Sunday school teacher, Mrs. Ruth Chambers of Stouffville, Ontario, Canada, who saw my interest and love for the poetry of Annie Johnson Flint. As a treasure of my own, Ruth gave me *Songs of Grace and Glory*, one of Annie's beautiful volumes of poetry. It is a tiny book that fits into my purse but one that I still read with great delight and pleasure to this day. Over the years, Annie's style has deeply influenced my life, as well as my writings.

The great author and pioneer missionary to India, Amy Carmichael, is a spiritual hero to me. Her devotional writings come out of the honest sharing from her heart and are especially suited for those experiencing trial and suffering. What God accomplished through her life has ministered deeply to my own soul.

As a consequence, the Lord also used Amy's life and style of writing to help me hear the call of the Saviour on my life and pursue a growing personal desire to write for Him. Eventually that included using my God-given talent to draw and paint for His glory by illustrating this volume of work.

I am thankful for the encouragement from family and loved ones: in particular, for my own dear mother, Mrs. Frances Spence, also a published author who enjoys prose. Over my lifetime, Mom has always encouraged me to grow in my talents. Her excitement and enthusiasm for every little creative effort is a continual boost to my heart.

For William and Sarah Howlett, my dear father- and mother-in-law, now with their Lord: Mom Howlett, for listening to my first feeble attempts at writing poetry. She lovingly and patiently guided me through some of the basic technical skills in how to present a clear rhyming message. Dad Howlett, for showering me with tender and loving support each step of the way, and for the godly example of sacrificial love that he set before us all. Together, their contribution and influence have been so significant that it is difficult to imagine how this book could have been realized without them. We know God is blessing them for their faithfulness to Him.

For Mrs. Olive Bazett-Jones, who appreciates and writes poetry as well. Olive and her husband Art were the faithful field representatives for Back To The Bible ministries from 1979 to 1988. After reading some of my early pieces, Olive encouraged me to write what God put in my heart and then to share it with the world.

For my dear "lifetime friend," Mrs. Ruth Ball, also the subject of the story "Birthday Cards Sent From God!" (pg. 120). She lovingly prays and encourages me, as a person, a friend and a sister-in-the-Lord. Her responses have taught me to listen not only with my heart but to write with my heart. For her patience in reading this material, offering honest thoughts and recommendations, my thanks are continual.

There are so many others who should be thanked: my very dear friends, Mrs. Roberta Hooper, Mrs. Doreen Marley, Doug and Mary Turner—special volunteer editors whose fellowship, friendship, perspective and helpful advice I value. For the many who have blessed us by their prayers or financial gifts, influenced and even inspired various writings and devotionals, whose names I may never know—but God knows and will bless abundantly—I thank you all.

For the amazing technical and literary training tools made available to me over the years, those instructional books from not only personal libraries but also public libraries at my disposal, for all such institutions I am grateful.

Though I never personally met her, there is another sister-in-the-Lord I can never forget. She purchased one of my framed poems, "Ambush, Earthquakes and Blooming In The Dark!" (pg. 128), from The Treasure House in Barrie, Ontario, in 1995. The story that sifted back to me through the store manager proved to be one that brought great personal blessing and needed encouragement. As a result, my heart was strengthened to continue believing that God had indeed called me to this work and would use it to bless the lives of others.

I realized afresh that when I allow the Lord to use every circumstance in my daily walk with Him, God will, in turn, multiply the comfort with which He comforts me from His Word. His is a tender watch care.

Without the love and prayerful support of my dear husband Ross and the many practical and mundane duties he faithfully performed, I could never have pursued this work of love. He, too, took valuable time from his studies to read and offer many sought-after suggestions in editing that were honest and insightful. I could not have seen this dream come true without his wisdom.

Ross continues to be my constant inspiration in writing disciplines, in honest sharing of the heart, in accuracy of belief and doctrine that remains true to God's Word, and in a glad obedience of my will to all that God calls me to do. I will always treasure his true and loving support. Ross always manages to keep me smiling with his delightful sense of humour. He is a special gift in my life from our Lord, and I am blessed.

Finally, God used His Living, Holy Word, the greatest book of all times, not only to transform my life but also to make clear His call to my heart to write. In particular, God used Isaiah's record, in chapter 38:9-20, where young King Hezekiah wrote down the blessings of God, both in times of good and times of suffering. He did this all with the express purpose of bringing God glory. This too is my desire.

This, with the victorious testimonies of Amy Carmichael's writings throughout her twenty years in a bed of deep suffering, illumined my heart further. I, too, was experiencing illness and suffering, but I wanted to obey God's calling and use the lessons learned in those trials by dedicating the talents and gifts He had given me for His Kingdom. I was weak and untrained, but I knew from God's promises that I could do all things through Christ who strengthens me (Philippians 4:13).

So it is clear that without God's direction and divine help this book would not be in your hands. To Him be all the glory and honour.

This is a work of love and joy. It is now a deep privilege to be able to share *The Treasure Of His Company* with you. May God be your Saviour and your Treasure today. There is nothing more precious than belonging to the Lord Jesus and, therefore, being able to look forward to enjoying Him for all Eternity. In that wonderful day we too will be a part of His precious treasure!

Thank You, dear Lord, for everything!

*O come, let us worship and bow down:*
*let us kneel before the LORD our maker.*
*For he is our God; and we are*
*the people of his pasture, and the sheep of his hand.*

(Psalm 95:6,7)

# Foreword

Often when one is invited to review a book the reader may not be personally acquainted with the author. In this case it is for me a great privilege to know the author and to confirm that what Jan writes is a true projection of her own sweet spirit and of her profound dedication to her Saviour and Lord. *The Treasure of His Company* is a delightful collection of real-life stories, meaningful poems and the author's own beautiful watercolours. She has a superb way of taking common everyday occurrences and transforming them into short, fascinating parables, always using the biblical text as a solid background.

She is vividly aware of today's world of sin and suffering, of violence and war, yet offers helpful prescriptions for our internal struggles. Her use of valuable quotes from such well-known writers as Charles Haddon Spurgeon, Amy Carmichael, Isobel Kuhn, A.W. Tozer, and John MacArthur, represents a fine selectivity. Her own insights are significant, particularly in her penetrating descriptions of our phobias and the emotional paralysis that stems from discouragements often inflicted on us by unthinking people. Tragedies and testings are set in the context of God's ultimate purposes for His people.

Central to all of this, of course, is the life, death and resurrection of the Lord Jesus from whom comes spiritual strength channelled to us by the Holy Spirit day by day. As Christ's suffering eventuated in glorious triumph, so the Christian is to travel the same pathway of perseverance and overcoming. Jan's meditations reach their climax in her vivid scriptural description of the wonder of the New Jerusalem and the sheer glory of God's Heaven.

Welcome, dear Reader, to a thrilling adventure of faith, hope and love, scaling mountaintop peaks and enjoying the valley experiences out of which emanate obedience, patience and true spirituality. This book will assure you that Jesus is with us all the way, until at last we become like Him—conformed to His blessed image!

> Dr. Arthur Paterson Lee,
> Pastor Emeritus and Author of
> *Three Faiths, One Father*
> *The Controversial Jesus and the Critics* &
> *Justice: Jesus and the Jews.*

# Preface

As I was preparing this collection of devotional messages and poetry, the words of a formal wedding invitation caught my attention. The proud parents of the bride requested the "pleasure of my company" and that we share in their day of joy. The picture behind that message wonderfully fit the heart of this work and thus the title, *The Treasure of His Company*, was born.

I thought of the grand Heavenly Invitation from the Father to each one of us to become part of the family that makes up the Body and Bride of Christ, the Church. The acceptance of that invitation ensures me that I will enjoy that appointed day at the Marriage Supper of the Lamb. "Treasured Invitation" (pg. 30) embraces this thought.

Until that Wedding day arrives, I can and do enjoy the precious treasure of His company, not only day by day but moment by moment.

Many devotional books and beautifully published works of poetry exist today, yet each volume stands on its own. This particular work grew out of a time of trial in my life when I began to record some of the precious blessings that came from my daily walk with my dear Lord and Saviour, Jesus Christ.

By faith, I put into verse the treasure that I discovered during those sweet encounters of the heart. And it is my prayer that you will not only be encouraged, but that your faith will be sweetened and strengthened. Then as your walk and life is stamped with the treasured intimacy of Christ's character and glory, you can know that you are bringing God joy. This is especially needful as we journey through the final pages of history, as we await the imminent return of Christ for His Bride, the Church.

How rich and glorious it is to share in such a privileged inheritance. If Christ Jesus is your Lord and you are watching for His coming, then it is also likely that you know what tests of faith and suffering are all about, what it is to endure hardship of every kind. You may well then identify with many of the poems and writings in this book, or you may know of those who could be girded up and renewed as you share this volume with them. It is also my prayer that you will find comfort from the Lord with which to comfort; joy with which to share joy; and, yes, hope with which to strengthen hope; all are blessings enjoyed by a true child of God. How wonderful to be in right standing, cleansed, forgiven, declared righteous, and, praise God, accepted in the Beloved forever!

The challenge before us is continual: to be found faithful until He comes. When we belong to the Lord Jesus, by faith in the finished work of Christ on Calvary's Cross, then we have great joy as we share and bask in what is now indeed only a foretaste of—

# The Treasure of His Company!

*May God be praised,*

***Jan Howlett***
Feeding His Lambs Ministries
Orillia, Ontario, Canada.

For where your treasure is, there will your heart be also.

(Matthew 6:21)

# Introduction

It has been a delight for me to read Jan Howlett's book of poems and to sense her deep appreciation for God's guiding hand in her life.

This book of poems is well named *The Treasure of His Company*, for one cannot read these pages without sensing that this woman writer enjoys a daily walk with God.

Rev. John Keble the 19th-century poet and hymn-writer who gave us the famous hymn "Sun of My Soul! Thou Saviour Dear" said, "Poetry, native and true poetry, is nothing less than each poet's innermost feeling issuing in rhythmic language."

In this lovely collection of Jan's poems, we have her inspired innermost feelings resulting in true poetry that brings before its readers the timeless truths of the Word of God. A few moments spent in these pages will be sure to brighten one's day and deepen one's faith.

> Dr. John M. Moore,
> International Evangelist, Bible Teacher, Pastor,
> Writer of over 150 Hymns & Choruses,
> Including "Burdens Are Lifted At Calvary"
> & "Why?"
> Author of *Plug Into Power* &
> *The Challenge of 1st Century Christianity.*
> His most recent book is *My Songs* & *Their Stories.*

*Thou wilt shew me the path of life:*
*in thy presence*
*is fulness of joy;*
*at thy right hand*
*there are pleasures for evermore.*

(Psalm 16:11)

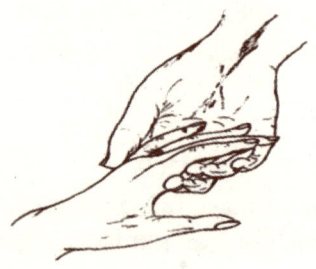

*...that in all things he [Jesus]*
*might have the preeminence.*

(Colossians 1:18)

# The Treasure Of His Company

# Treasured Invitation

"Glorious Journey"

Jesus saith unto him,
I am the way, the truth, and the life:
no man cometh unto the Father, but by me.

(John 14:6)

# Treasured Invitation

It was a warm sunny day—the kind when nothing could fail—
When my own Invitation arrived with the morning mail.
An elegant envelope, engraved with baby blue larks,
The paper itself glistened with tiny pearls and pink hearts.

Wedding invitations always bring a special affair
Where family and friends celebrate the day with great flair;
Requesting "the pleasure of your company" for the bride,
Proud parents announce the marriage with great joy and deep pride.

Yes, a great honour to be found on such an elite list,
And so we would not let this occasion pass or be missed!
Our reply must be sent, and a lovely gift to be bought,
Much planning with great excitement consumes much of our thought!

They stand as one now, with God's Word as their Staff and their Rod.
And as we witness their promised vows of love unto God,
Deep within our hearts we too renew our vows with a pledge;
Sweet memories tell us that this too was our privilege.

My thoughts whirling back to the card sitting now before me
Spoke to my heart of God's Word—like beautiful poetry—
How Jesus defeated my sin, and the Invitation
For His Bride to enjoy the Marriage Feast Celebration.

The Invitation in my hand to this earthly wedding
Spoke of a future day—where I should also be heading.
But I wondered, was my name written on God's Divine list?
Would He invite? For His Love, I could no longer resist.

Yet, could it be true? Is it real? Am I reading aright?
God requested my answer; indeed for this very night!
Clearly, in beautiful handwritten script, slightly inset—
There was *my* name, and words I shall never, ever forget!

Surrounded by diamonds, jewels and rich borders of gold,
Those precious, kind words set apart just for me would enfold
Not just my heart, my will or my love, but my everything—
But what could I do in return?—What could I do? But sing!

For this amazing Invitation was straight from Glory,
And the message of God's dear Love had written my story.
For Jesus Himself was the Groom; the Bride I could just see
But lo and behold, what I saw was too precious for me.

Then, out of that Light, came a voice filled with amazing Love,
"Precious you are now, and your life will fit Mine like a glove,
Father requests 'the pleasure of your company,' dear child;
He longs each day to share, for to Me, you are reconciled.

"Yes, My Plan was set in place—the Gift bought so long ago.
For now where your treasure is, there will your heart be also."
When I replied, "Oh, yes, dear Lord Jesus: I *will* be yours!"
Angel music unfurled Heaven's gates and opened the doors!

Rainbows of light shone over the Gates of gold and pearl,
And standing, His Wedding Robe draped on His arm in a swirl,
Was the Bridegroom—My Saviour—His hand lovingly outstretched
Calling to our hearts, from the Book of Life each name He fetched.

Each soul in my daydream waited for God's Will to fulfill,
When all of a sudden, now as time completely stood still,
Christ made His choice, and one by one at last we could all see,

The *Treasured Invitation* was sent—
to you—
And—To me!

> He who dwells in the shelter
> of the Most High
> will rest in the shadow of the Almighty.
> I will say of the LORD,
> "He is my refuge and my fortress,
> my God, in whom I trust."
>
> (Psalm 91:1,2 NIV)

## From Such Treasures, Flee!

Is your treasure where your heart will dwell?
A place where moth and rust cannot fell,
Destroy, crush, despite all time and stress—
Or is your hoard earning less and less?
Will it endure through Eternity?
If not, from such treasures run—yes, flee!
Better to dwell with a "heart contented"
Than with prayers, treasures circumvented.
Can you answer honestly tonight,
That your treasure is in Him, sealed tight?

# The Secret Place of Heart's Content!
*For where your treasure is, there will your heart be also.*
(Matthew 6:21)

It was an extremely hot, muggy afternoon. But, unlike most folks who were outside enjoying the summer day, I was inside melting in the heat, overwhelmed with many burdens. As the day wore on they only seemed to multiply as I listened to the noon-hour newscast. The reports of continual violence, immorality and nations on the brink of world war reminded me, in stark terms, of the effect that sin has had on the world.

I'm certain we have all had days when it seemed as if there would be no end to the noise and the distress, no peace and no refuge and no contentment to be found anywhere. This was certainly one of those days for me, and I did not feel at all content. Amy Carmichael, missionary to India, called such days "wormy" in her book *Rose From Brier*. If only I could get away from all of this not-so-lovely reality and find relief from my own storm.

I breathed a silent prayer asking my Heavenly Father to help me to snap out of these nagging, discouraging thoughts and to focus on something with eternal purpose.

I tried to relax and enjoy a soothing cup of tea. I was supposed to be writing a thank-you note, but I just sat staring at the grey rug. It was quite some time before some colourful text on the cover of a borrowed travel guide sitting on the coffee table halted my gaze. Without too much thought I picked it up and mindlessly thumbed through a few pages, hoping to get some easy, quick relief. It was not until I came across a long-forgotten, richly coloured antique map that my interest awakened. I was completely fascinated with the unique names of the towns and cities, many of which I had never heard of before that day. Within minutes I actually began to feel less sad, and somehow my heavy spirit seemed lighter.

I followed the coastline of the island on the map as city after city drew me in. Finally, one city was such a surprise that I exclaimed out loud, "Oh, what a lovely place for a family to live!"

Wonderful cities like Angel's Cove and Chapel Arm, as well as special towns where children might be heard laughing and giggling, called Tickle Harbor and Sunnyside! Doesn't that paint a lovely picture?

Another area known as Trinity Bay was embraced by a trio of cities: Heart's Delight, Heart's Desire and a place I am certain all of us would long to call home, known as Heart's Content. Each city was nestled safely among several quaint churches.

I tried to imagine what it was about the land and their experience that caused the settlers to name each city after a condition of the heart. Indeed, it was a picture of quiet tranquillity, safety, refuge and well-being. As you can well imagine I immediately wanted to pack my bags and take up residence in those delightful, faraway places to escape all of my distress.

But, I reasoned, surely these dreamlike places only exist in fairy tales. Yet this travel guide clearly depicted them on the map of Canada in the Avalon Peninsula of Newfoundland! How comforting to think such places truly existed, but I needed to know more about this grand island.

As I read the article I was surprised to learn that this same island continually braved battered shores, wild and unpredictable ocean storms and dense fog, as well as many rainy, dull and misty days.

On the coastline—often threatened by terrible and frightening storms—but not too far inland were these places of apparent refuge, peace, joy and safety. Just like the Secret Place, I thought. And, wasn't that the focus of my Scripture reading in Psalm 91 this morning, where it described the Secret Place so beautifully?

I closed the travel guide and finished my last sip of tea. My thoughts continued to mull over this new discovery and, in particular, the city called Heart's Content. I realized that living in Ontario, Canada, would not and could not duplicate or begin to provide the apparent or imagined blessings of the inviting, faraway city called Heart's Content.

I also knew that if this city truly lived up to its name, then in order for me to enjoy those same blessings, I would, in fact, have to personally live in the city of Heart's Content in Newfoundland, not in Orillia, Ontario; for the city of Heart's Content did not exist in Orillia but it did in Newfoundland.

Indeed, these cities had portrayed a lovely haven, but they had also illustrated some important biblical truths, just when I so needed them—truths I knew well but truths that the cares of the day had crowded out.

First of all, the spiritual refuge and contentment that I needed and sought and the idyllic picture painted by the cities in the travel guide could never provide that perfect, lasting contentment or that eternal refuge, because only God Himself could provide such a place! But they could and did redirect my focus.

Secondly, true contentment, eternal refuge and peace can only be found and enjoyed, first and foremost, when we accept Jesus Christ as our own personal Lord and Saviour. I belong to the Lord, so those promises are mine. Indeed, they are my foundation.

Then, thirdly, our joy continues as we live for Christ in His Presence, in sweet fellowship together, day by day, moment by moment, keeping our gaze fixed on Him. Clearly, I had lost my focus.

So when we face great storms in our lives, we need to remember Psalm 91. It is in that psalm that we discover that the Shelter of Peace for which we long is in Jesus Christ, The Prince of Peace. He is the "Secret Place of the Most High." And it is there in the Secret Place that we discover afresh the *Treasure* of His company.

Of course, we do not come to enjoy the gifts of peace or spiritual contentment and refuge by simply reading, memorizing or quoting this famous psalm, word for word. No, it is only as we get to know the Divine Author, personally, that the promises become a living reality for each of us.

Wherever I live, geographically, whether in Newfoundland or in Ontario, in a faraway city or on a foreign continent, it matters not. I dwell with Christ in the Secret Place, because He indwells my heart.

I had allowed the burdens of the day to quickly crowd out the very remedy I had read about when I started my day but had failed to apply. It was a *heart* issue.

What a lesson! Yes, my burdens and concerns still existed, but I knew Who could handle them, and I placed them back into His hands. Nothing could disturb or steal my joy. Finally I could face the rest of the day, eager to serve the Lord in any little task He lay before me, for I had found true Heart's Content in the Secret Place, just as Psalm 91 had promised.

# The Secret Place of Heart's Content!

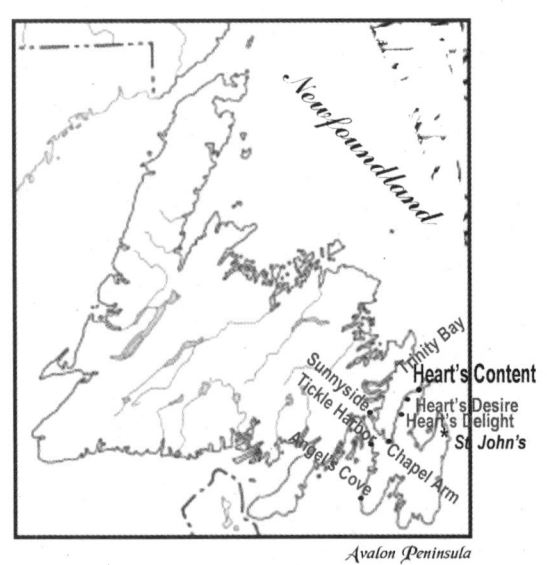

*Avalon Peninsula*

*For where your treasure is,
there will your heart be also.*

(Matthew 6:21)

*Thy word is a lamp
unto my feet,
and a light
unto my path.*

*(Psalm 119:105)*

## A Lamp And A Light

*Whether it is by day or night,
God's Word is a lamp and a light
Shining bright to lead me along—
In my life, my walk and in my song.*

*"Truth cannot be contradicted with truth; it can only be denounced with falsehood."*

Dr. John MacArthur, Jr.

Taken from *The MacArthur New Testament Commentary: Matthew 8-15*, by John MacArthur, Moody Publishers, © 1985, p. 103. Used by permission.

For this is what the LORD says—
he who created the heavens,
he is God;
he who fashioned and made the earth,
he founded it... "I am the LORD, and there is no other...
I, the LORD, speak the truth; I declare what is right."
(Isaiah 45:18,19 NIV)

# Psalm 91 NIV

He who dwells in the shelter of the Most High
will rest in the shadow of the Almighty.
I will say of the LORD, "He is my refuge and my fortress,
my God, in whom I trust."
Surely He will save you from the fowler's snare
and from the deadly pestilence.
He will cover you with his feathers,
and under his wings you will find refuge;
His faithfulness will be your shield and rampart.
You will not fear the terror of night,
nor the arrow that flies by day,
nor the pestilence that stalks in the darkness,
nor the plague that destroys at midday.
A thousand may fall at your side,
ten thousand at your right hand,
but it will not come near you.
You will only observe with your eyes
and see the punishment of the wicked.
If you make the Most High your dwelling—
even the LORD, who is my refuge—
then no harm will befall you,
no disaster will come near your tent.
For he will command his angels concerning you
to guard you in all your ways;
they will lift you up in their hands,
so that you will not strike your foot against a stone.
You will tread upon the lion and the cobra;
you will trample the great lion and the serpent.
"Because he loves me," says the LORD, "I will rescue him;
I will protect him, for he acknowledges my name.
He will call upon me, and I will answer him;
I will be with him in trouble,
I will deliver him and honor him.
With long life will I satisfy him
and show him my salvation."

# By Special Request!

*Behold the Lamb of God,
which taketh away the sin
of the world.*

*(John 1:29)*

*God has given us eternal life, and
this life is in his Son.
He who has the Son has life;
he who does not have the Son of God
does not have life.*

*(1 John 5:11,12 NIV*

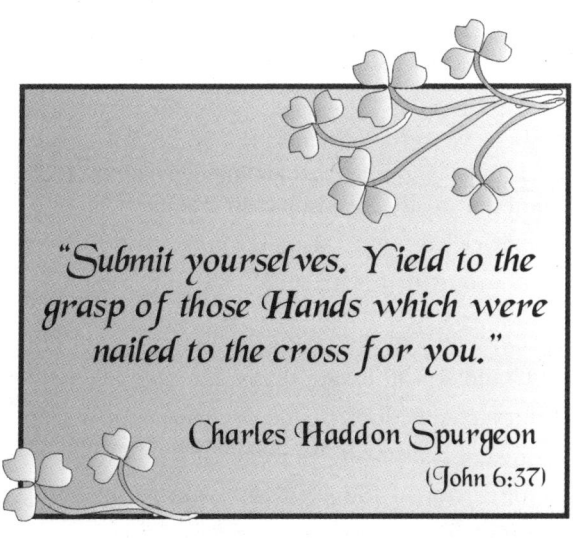

"Submit yourselves. Yield to the grasp of those Hands which were nailed to the cross for you."

Charles Haddon Spurgeon
(John 6:37)

Taken from Metropolitan Tabernacle Pulpit, Sermon No. 1, 910, p.396.
The Banner of Truth Trust, Carlisle, P.A. Used by permission.

## Yield To His Grasp

Clearly, there is no better place or perfect time to yield
One's entire life and soul—to overcome sin's battlefield.
Then at last, from your turmoil you can triumphantly cease,
As you receive complete forgiveness and eternal peace.
Yes, when you surrender by faith, Christ's love transforms anew,
In the grasp of His Hands, which were nailed
to the Cross—for you.

# By Special Request!
*(Original story heard in a sermon many years ago: Source unknown)*

Somewhere in England, now lost to history past,
A crowd settled themselves while the stage was cast.
Among their great company, one special man,
Known to all—loved by each and every fan—
They called him to share his great gift to recite;
To favour them with special requests tonight!

After a lull, an aged pastor arose,
"Could you sir, recite Psalm 23, God's Prose?"
But a strange look passed over the actor's face,
Pausing a moment, his reply came with grace.
"Yes, I can—I will—but with your permission
You recite it as well—my one condition."

\* \* \* \*

Impressively the actor began the psalm;
His voice painting various pictures of calm,
Then lifting to heights that would thrill and excite,
He stirred minds and ears with dramatic delight!
Yes, his audience was completely spellbound
As thundering applause and praise shook the ground.

Then the pastor quietly stood to his feet,
His voice, not one you would expect could compete.
Though his expression faltered, he could be heard,
But as he began, he simply spoke God's Word.
No sound, no loud applause broke out in shrillness,
Just a deafening awe filled all that stillness!

When he had finished, not a word was spoken,
Hearts and heads bowed in the hush yet unbroken;
Still smitten and moved, they were deeply distraught.
Before they extolled the actor without thought,
But this was distinct—it could not be explained—
They waited in reverence while silence reigned.

\*\*\*\*

At last the actor stood to his feet, shaking,
His voice quite emotional, and still quaking.
He laid his hand on the minister's shoulder
And turned to the people—wiser and older.
He waited just a moment to clear his throat;
Catching their attention, added this footnote.

"The difference, you wonder?—It is just this—
The 23rd Psalm, not one word did I miss.
Yes, I know it by rote—still I missed the goal.
I reached your eyes and your ears, but not your soul!
But now this dear man touched your hearts with
  God's Word.
Yes, I know the psalm—
                **But, he knows**
                    **The Shepherd!"**

*I am the good shepherd; I know my sheep
and my sheep know me...
My sheep listen to my voice...and they follow me.*

(John 10:14,27 NIV)

"The great message of the Gospel, and therefore of the church, is not a call to morality but a call to deliverance from sin through the Lord Jesus Christ."

Dr. John MacArthur, Jr.

Taken from *The MacArthur New Testament Commentary: Matthew 8-15*, by John MacArthur, Moody Publishers, © 1985, p. 340. Used by permission.

"Who could be careless about sin with Calvary in view? It is not by looking at sin that we see it for what it is, but by looking at the love of God and His pure holiness. As we look at that we begin to understand something of... the nature of sin."

Amy Carmichael

Taken from *Gold By Moonlight*, Amy Carmichael, Christian Literature Crusade © 1935, p. 58. Used by permission.

# God's Salvation Gift!

*For the wages of sin is death; but the gift of God is eternal life through Jesus Christ our Lord.*

(Romans 6:23)

# God's Salvation Gift!
## Revelation 20:11-15; Psalm 56:8; Daniel 7:10;12:1; Malachi 3:16,17a

God has many books, but only one Lamb's Book of Life.
The lost He must judge by His Word, the two-edged knife.
So when your own hour of death comes, will you be in doubt?
Is your name written therein, or is it blotted out?
Why miss God's heaven and the Presence of the Saviour?
Come to know Jesus Christ; He will change your behaviour.

"For God so loved the world that He gave His only Son."
Christ, the sacrificial Lamb, has all the battle won!
There is nothing we can offer—work out or become.
To gain Salvation, accept His gift, which is wisdom.
Confess you are a sinner and need a life-Saver;
Christ will present you faultless and stand in your favour!

His Gospel gives all the answers and the Way is paved,
"Believe now on the Lord Jesus Christ and be thou saved."
Trust in Him without delay, before it is too late;
Doubting men who refuse God's Truth leave it all to fate.
His blood paid our debt in full. It's up to you to choose
But reject Him, and your Salvation Gift you will lose!

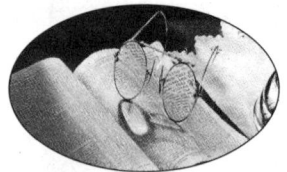

*For God so loved the world, that he gave his only begotten Son, that whosoever believeth in him should not perish, but have everlasting life.*

(John 3:16)

*Now is the accepted time;*
*behold,*
*now is the day*
*of salvation.*

(2 Corinthians 6:2)

*"But though we cannot by our own act*
*lift ourselves out of the pit,*
*we must by an act of our own*
*take hold of the hand*
*which offers us out of it."*

J.C. Augustus Hare
Guesses At Truth

Taken from *Flowers Along The Path*, Esther Carls Dodgen,
Barbour Publishing Inc. © 2001, p. 48. Used with permission.

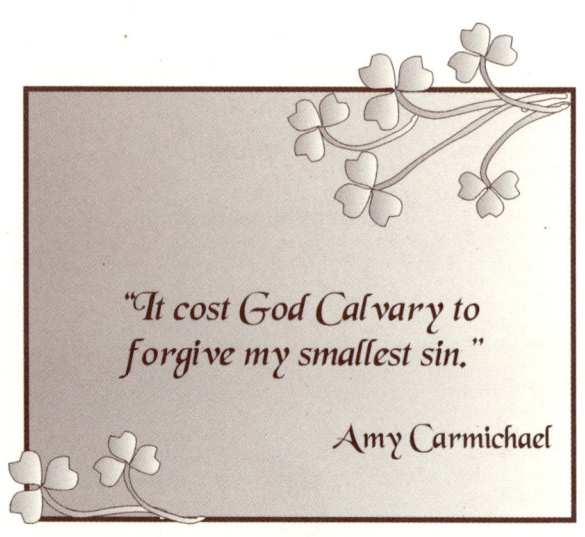

"It cost God Calvary to forgive my smallest sin."

Amy Carmichael

Taken from *Edges of His Way*, by Amy Carmichael, Christian Literature Crusade, © 1984, p. 33. Used by permission.

## No Small Thing?

Just a small thing, you say so carelessly;
But just one sin still declares us guilty.
So how could such a tiny thing separate
Our hearts from Almighty God Incarnate?
God's Word says all have sinned and fallen short;
Our sin cost God the Cross—our death to thwart—
His Love and tender Mercy, can I know?
**Yes, to the foot of Calvary we can go!**

# Washed In The Blood of The Lamb

And from Jesus Christ, who is the faithful witness,
and the first begotten of the dead,
and the prince of the kings of the earth.
Unto him that loved us, and
washed us from our sins in his own blood,
And hath made us kings and priests
unto God and his Father;
to him be glory and dominion for ever and ever.
Amen.

(Revelation 1:5,6)

# Washed In The Blood Of The Lamb
## "The Gift of Life"

It was a place whose name spoke of death and evil. It was stained with the blood of both the guilty and the innocent. This place was the epitome of the world's most notorious seat of torture and hate. And today, evil reached its pinnacle as a thick veil of heavy darkness shrouded the hill of Golgotha, known as "the Place of the Skull." Indeed, the darkest night had fallen over this place, yet it was still the middle of the day. Truly this gruesome hill was not the picture of love, or rest, or peace or hope. That is—not until today!

But He Who was all of these lovely virtues hung lifeless and forsaken on Golgotha's cross. To many it appeared that the Lord Jesus Christ had been silenced and the Light of the world extinguished forever.

How much more the added impact of hopelessness would now be felt in the midst of this unexplained blackness. It was impossible to grope or move about safely, or to breathe—the air was so thick. Everyone was surrounded by these wild elements, yet Almighty God was in complete control. Forced to turn His face away from His beloved Son, God poured out His wrath upon sin, indeed, upon the sins of the whole world—my sin and your sin—all was laid upon Jesus who knew no sin. What unspeakable agony!

The eerie darkness filled hearts with terrible dread. The earth continued to rumble. Earthquakes shook the ground until the graves of dead men, finally, gave up their treasure to God.

And then, at last it seemed quiet and a sense of stillness crept over the place, as if the world was holding its breath. Ancient prophecies had been completed and fulfilled. Victory over sin and death had been won, once and for all. It was over.

I imagined in my heart that all of Heaven must have wept bitterly. Although the following scene was the creation of a screenwriter's imagination, God used it to awaken my tired heart to realize afresh the great depth of God's Love for me. His sacrificial provision to redeem my lost soul cost Him everything.

In one of Hollywood's made-for-television films, the scene was portrayed dramatically as the rains descended and flowed down the wooden stake that held the body of the beloved Christ, the Saviour of the world. Rolling thunder, frightening displays of sheet lightning and bolts of fierce electricity seared through the sky—air to ground, ground to air—making the heavens seem alive with an indescribable power.

As I watched, the flow of rain washed over the Cross and the bloodstained body of my dear Saviour, His blood so willingly shed and His life so lovingly given—His life for mine, for yours. It drained down to the ground, pooled at the foot of the Cross, breaking over its hill as if washing over my own feet and finally disappeared beyond the embankment. In that exact moment, I cried out in anguish. My heart was breaking as I choked back the tears, overwhelmed afresh with love and gratitude. I prayed, "Thank you, dear Jesus, for truly washing me in the Blood of the Lamb, for cleansing me and for forgiving me of all my sins. Thank you for making me Your child."

I cried like a lost child, remembering what it was like to have been rescued from the dark. I had seen my deep need of a Saviour, confessed my sin and given my heart to Jesus so many years ago. I had become a brand new person with a new purpose for my life. But tonight, although I cried until I was spent, I was at peace because I was filled with His love.

This ugly Place of the Skull was Calvary, but for me it was a place that had been completely transformed. My sin had been forever conquered. Truly the Gift of Life was offered to all, but I also knew that Jesus died in my place—the very place where I should have been—and now I owed my life to Him. But that was only the beginning. The Lord Jesus Christ rose from the dead, and He is seated at the right hand of the Father, interceding for you and for me today.

The Bible says "*now is the day of salvation*" (2 Corinthians 6:2). But are you washed in the blood of the Lamb? Dear one, will you also accept the Gift He has purchased for you with His own lifeblood? Oh, what a Gift! What a Saviour! What a Salvation! Indeed, He is The Gift of Life!

If you do not yet know Him as your own personal Lord and Saviour, then please don't put this decision off any longer. Remember, Jesus loved you enough to die for you, and He rose up from the dead to give each of us New Life—Eternal Life! Now, because He lives, we can sing that dear old hymn with new joy and great vigour, "Are you washed in the blood of the Lamb?"—and you will be able to answer with complete certainty, "Yes!"

*For we preach not ourselves,
but Christ Jesus the Lord;
and ourselves your servants
for Jesus' sake.
For God, who commanded the light
to shine out of darkness,
hath shined in our hearts,
to give the light of the knowledge
of the glory of God
in the face of Jesus Christ.*

(2 Corinthians 4:5,6)

"Never let what you know be distressed
by what you do not know."

Amy Carmichael

Taken from *Gold By Moonlight*, Amy Carmichael,
Christian Literature Crusade ©1935 p. 127. Used by permission.

# Honour And Remembrance

*But we have this treasure in earthen vessels,
that the excellency of the power
may be of God, and not of us.*

(2 Corinthians 4:7)

# Honour And Remembrance
## Freedom And Redemption

As long as men and women live on this earth, the images and ghosts of war can never be forgotten. The scars of terror and trauma that brave soldiers endured are often seen in photographs neatly arranged on mantles and coffee tables: things that were almost unimaginable to those of us who have never seen war but continue to enjoy blood-bought freedom!

In our day with "real-time war," raw twenty-four-hour "on-air" battlefield reporting, we are brought up short. We realize, as never before, just how the price of freedom from seen and unseen enemies, and those bent on sin and evil, cuts to the heart. War affects every one of us past, present and future.

As a younger generation, generally speaking, world war is something that we have never experienced. We are humbled and compelled to fall to our knees, silenced to all other thought but to pray for our dedicated men and women who are in the thick of battle today. As they serve, they sacrifice all comforts to maintain our privilege of peace and freedom and to protect the world from debauchery. Indeed, we honour our Forces, the living and the dead, whose blood was spilled to give us liberty.

Yet, there is another Liberty that was won for us by One greater than all brave soldiers. That One, as some of those same soldiers would agree, is the Lord Jesus Christ. He, whose Holy Blood was poured out on our behalf, also willingly gave up His own will to restore us to Himself. Jesus did this so that we could be free from sin for all eternity. He demonstrated this sacrificial Love even when we would not acknowledge Him as Saviour.

If Jesus had not stepped in to bridge the gap for sin—to provide us with the opportunity to receive spiritual redemption and reconciliation—we could never know lasting or eternal peace of any kind. The soldiers we honour today could not redeem us from the sin that separates us from God or those sins that cause evil and deadly wars. But they have, with God on their side, won earthly freedoms. Only God offers the Gift of Life, and if we accept that gift, He grafts us into Himself. And when we are grafted in, eternal peace and freedom are ours.

There is yet another host and another great cloud of witnesses, composed of those faithful martyrs who have died on the battlefield for their faith in Christ, martyrs who grace the halls of Heaven and whom we, as the Church, also honour. These were the soldiers for the Kingdom of God, an army whose robes have been washed in the blood of the Lamb. The many who have gone before us we honour by being, in turn, faithful. We are not worthy of these great soldiers of the Cross.

Yes, a great debt has been paid. When it comes to the model of sacrifice, you and I must first honour the Saviour, for He gave His all when He died in our place. When we honour Him first, we can honestly and respectfully stand and honour our brave men and women as we ought. We can do it with a deeper understanding of what they won on our behalf, for, in a sense, whether realized or not, they tried to follow His great example.

*If we say that we have fellowship with Him and
yet walk in the darkness, we lie and
do not practice the truth;
but if we walk in the light as He Himself is in the light,
we have fellowship with one another,
and the blood of Jesus His Son cleanses us from all sin.*

*If we say that we have no sin,
we are deceiving ourselves
and the truth is not in us.
If we confess our sins,
He is faithful and righteous to forgive us our sins
and to cleanse us from all unrighteousness.*

(1 John 1:6–9 NASB)

# Honour And Remembrance

In the distance, a weary-hearted soldier, home on leave,
Stands mourning by a grave, this cold and dark Remembrance Eve.
He cannot help staring at the simple, white, wooden cross,
Realizing, across this yard now marks rows and rows of loss:
Symbols of sacrifice, sorrow, the giving up of life
To preserve their country's peace from this tired war and strife.

Though night shadows lengthen, grief only deepens and remains;
His cries form voiceless words as he breathes, "Who can heal these pains?"
Suddenly! As if in answer, thunderous lightning hits,
And, in half, an ancient oak tree completely cracks and splits!
But in that same instant, this sad young man falls to his knees
Choked and grieving now for the world's deep need for peace and ease.

With tear-filled eyes he slowly raised his head, only to see—
Divinely superimposed—there over that wounded tree,
A lonely shadow cast by the grave markers in that yard;
God reminded him of Christ's hands—for him—were deeply scarred.
There, fixed silently upon that grave, was Calvary's Cross;
That night he saw his own personal, spiritual loss!

He's no longer afraid of death's grave or this war-filled strife,
Because now his name is written in the Lamb's Book of Life!
Yes, he had true freedom from sin and spiritual death
When he received blood-bought Salvation as his life, his breath!
Yes, at this reflective time, we truly honour our dead,
But first honour the Saviour, for Jesus
        Died—**in your stead!**

*Peradventure for a good man some would even dare to die.*
*But God commendeth his love toward us, in that,*
*while we were yet sinners, Christ died for us.*

*(Romans 5:7,8)*

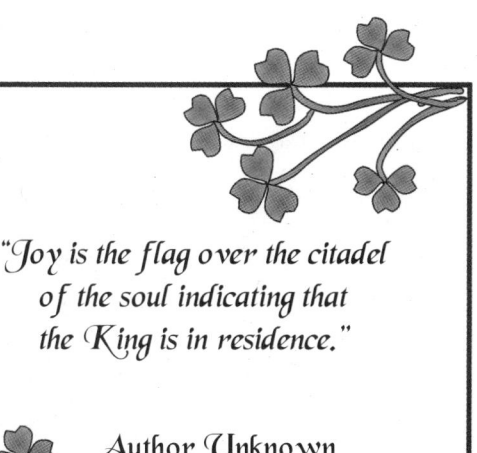

"Joy is the flag over the citadel
of the soul indicating that
the King is in residence."

Author Unknown

Taken from *Flowers Along The Path*, Esther Carls Dodgen,
Barbour Publishing, © 2001, p. 161. Used by permission.

"God often plants His flowers among rough rocks."

Author Unknown

# God's Precious Remembrance Book!
## Malachi 3: 16,17 NIV

ur dear Heavenly Father keeps a special written treasure, His Remembrance Book filled with praises for Christ beyond measure.

One of the many ways we delight our great Lord of Glory
Comes when the Church tells how much they love His Redemption Story!

How precious it is to God when His children express their love,
Worshipping His Name with praise-filled awe, exalting Christ above.

Yes, Jesus carved us in His hands, and His love still makes us whole.
The Father indwells our praise and records it all on His Scroll!

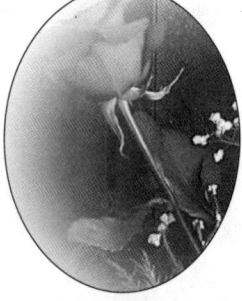

*Then those who feared the LORD talked with each other, and the LORD listened and heard. A scroll of remembrance was written in his presence concerning those who feared the LORD and honored his name.*

*"They will be mine," says the LORD Almighty, "in the day when I make up my treasured possession. I will spare them..."*

(Malachi 3:16,17 NIV)

# The Old Road Home

Thou wilt shew me the path of life:
in thy presence is fulness of joy;
at thy right hand there are pleasures for evermore.

(Psalm 16:11)

## God's Mercies Bring Joy

Yes, all God's Mercies are fresh each new sunrise,
And because of His Love, His Joy is my prize—
Just knowing that we will never be apart,
For Jesus has forgiven and cleansed my heart!

## The Old Road Home

Is it not wonderful to know that the "old road Home"
Is quite plain and direct, and does not aimlessly roam?
For Jesus travelled it long ago—meeting the day
Smoothing the rough, straightening the bent or crooked way.

Though the road is narrow, yet with Love it is strewn
With writings on landmarks and signposts carved and hewn
By our precious Saviour, whose Mercy counted the cost
To secure Salvation for *all* of us who were lost.

His Love covers us, so under His wings we can rest.
Jesus is our Refuge and Peace—He comforts us best!
God's Word tells us our final dwelling is not this earth,
For we are truly just strangers passing through since birth.

Assured the place He's prepared will not make us sorry
We are Heaven bound, ready to meet Christ in Glory.
So always live for Him, and from His Way never roam.
Don't miss out, **Yes Travel with me—**
                                on the "old road Home!"

> *Enter ye in at the strait gate:*
> *for wide is the gate, and broad is the*
> *way, that leadeth to destruction,*
> *and many there be which go in thereat:*
> *Because strait is the gate, and narrow is*
> *the way, which leadeth unto life,*
> *and few there be that find it.*
>
> *(Matthew 7:13,14)*

*He will cover you
with his feathers,
and under his wings
you will find refuge;
his faithfulness
will be your shield and rampart.*

(Psalm 91:4 NIV)

"Truth engages the citadel of the human heart
and is not satisfied until
it has conquered everything there.
The will must come forth and
surrender its sword."

A.W. Tozer
Of God and Men

Reprinted from *The Best of Tozer*, Compiled by
Warren Wiersbe, ©1978 by Christian Publication, Inc., p. 141.
Used with permission.

# Trusting The Arm of God

There have been many unique stories written and amazing pictures painted to illustrate and interpret the powerful, dynamic truth of what it means to experience complete peace and trust in the midst of great turmoil.

And then there are those other circumstances when we find ourselves in a lull, where there is no discernable disturbance or hint of activity, and when there may not be anything we can do but wait quietly and patiently: truly trusting the invisible arm of God.

For instance, Willy, my neighbour's cat, has developed his own personal ritual when he greets me. Because he has patiently waited for hours just for me to open the back door, he becomes quite excited and tries very hard to speed up the process. As far as he is concerned, he would rather forget the usual preliminaries now and get right to the snuggle routine on my lap.

Originally the process involved hellos and greetings at the door, the raising of his paws up to my knees, waiting for his pat on the head and then the go-ahead signal to position himself on the step, ready to jump up on my lap. Once he was up on his perch he would line himself up with my left arm, which was resting along the length of my lap. He would begin pushing hard along my arm with his head down, rump in the air, then flop down and curl up into a ball. The purring had already begun, and if the tip of his little pink tongue was protruding just a bit, I knew he was very content.

As Willy leaned his weight on my arm, he would be half on my lap and half off of my lap, so the only support holding him from completely falling a reasonable distance to the grass below was my left arm. His little body was actually being held up the entire time by my arm; if my arm were to grow too weak to hold him, he would, indeed, fall off! But because he trusted me and felt safe, he rested and enjoyed being in my presence. Although I knew what Willy really wanted was to be allowed to come into the house, nevertheless, he was content.

As I thought about how very trusting Willy was of my care to hold him safe, I thought of how much more my Heavenly Father loved me and was holding me in His strong arm, safe and sound.

His arm would never weaken; nor would it give way. It would never let me go, because I was trusting in Jesus as my Saviour.

Because He is my strong tower, I can trust Him for every circumstance in my life, whether in a fierce storm or in times of apparent motionless tracking. Often, those are the times when I may also wish that He would allow me to see hints of progress or movement on a matter concerning the future.

Nevertheless, I know I am safe. And like Willy, I can choose to enjoy His Presence and rest. I know, with great confidence, that the Lord is working behind the scenes and that He is carrying me when I cannot trace His footsteps. And when I can't trace His footsteps at times, I can trust God's Heart. What a blessing to realize that we belong to Him and that He is holding us secure every step of the way. No wonder, then, I can lean on Him, content, and trust my entire being to the strong Arm of God.

*[Hezekiah] spoke encouragingly to them, saying,*
*"Be strong and courageous, do not fear or be dismayed*
*because of the king of Assyria nor because of all the horde*
*that is with him; for the one with us is greater than the one*
*with him.*
*"With him is only an arm of flesh, but with us is the*
*LORD our God to help us and to fight our battles."*
*And the people relied on the words of Hezekiah king of Judah.*

(2 Chronicles 32:6,7,8 NASB)

"All God's giants have been weak men who did great things for God because they reckoned on God being with them."

Hudson Taylor

Taken from *Goforth of China*, Rosalind Goforth, © 1937, p. 210.

"When one door closes, another opens, but we often look so long and so regretfully upon the closed door that we do not see the one which has opened for us."

Alexander Graham Bell

# But Lord, Who Am I?

Plans for my blessing, like seedlings, rise to bloom and grow,
And though God nurtures each one, my doubts still ebb and flow.
My confusion still groans, "Is this God or just self-made?"
I pray, I wonder, "Will this fog cloud soon lift or fade?"
Though I can't yet fathom how God might myself employ,
Great anticipation is mixed with both fear and joy!

But when His simple plan unfolds, I'm still shocked to the core.
I gasp, "Lord—impossible!" Yet, God has moved the door.
Old doubts fan and feed the flames with brand new discontents,
It's as if I face insurmountable arguments.
Yet all at once, weaknesses converge and amplify;
Unbelief, self-doubt with fears, rise up and multiply.

Once my song was victorious, "Yes, Lord, here am I."
But now?—"No, Lord, who am I?"—becomes my lonely cry.
I'm left shaken, confused, and a part of me has died.
My peace is lost, dissolved, as I go against the tide.
But fear subsides, when I recall, by expedience,
God's gracious charge and my promise of obedience.

Then, when God's Will is clear to my heart and to my soul,
Peace restored, trusts with a trust that measures not its toll.
In just one precious moment, "My song," I must confess
"Who He Is"—*not* "Who am I?"—unveils my storm and stress.
Just the very place Satan would have me, victim, stall—
But, new joy and peace are mine,
> **When I obey**
> **God's Call!**

*And God said unto Moses...say...I AM has sent me unto you.*

(Exodus 3:14)

> "A crucified life and heart
> ...that is full of sweetness
> cannot spill bitter drops
> however sharply knocked."
>
> Amy Carmichael

Taken from *Gold By Moonlight*, Amy Carmichael, Christian Literature Crusade,  1935, p. 81. Used by permission.

Wash away all my iniquity and
cleanse me from my sin,
For I know my transgressions...

Create in me a pure heart, O God,
and renew a steadfast spirit within me.

The sacrifices of God are a broken spirit;
a broken and a contrite heart, O God,
you will not despise.

(Psalm 51: 2-3,10,17 NIV)

# Hannah's Desire

They shall call his name Emmanuel,
which being interpreted is, God with us.

(Matthew 1:23)

# Hannah's Desire
## I Samuel Ch. 1

Behold the life of Hannah characterized by grace,
Thoughts of God's glory and holiness glow in her face;
Radiating like butterflies, His beauties unfold,
Like delicate feathers, edged with lace and precious gold.
Such is the intricate handwork of our Father's plan,
This lovely creation made by God alone, not man.

It was not always so for this vessel under fire,
With dreams unfulfilled for just one personal desire.
But Hannah struggled and strained, still unable to trust;
Her worst fear—she would be left with just ashes and dust.
In the midst of broken dreams she could not give God praise,
But lived on in sorrow, misunderstanding His ways.

All these years childless, she wept with no hope of relief:
Weary in soul, ashamed, and so overwhelmed with grief.
Still barren and bruised, scornful words would just pierce and sting,
With no heart for praise, her life became a joyless thing.
Her days seemed so empty; her purpose—just tears and strife;
She could neither worship, feast or enjoy family life.

Years nurtured ugly roots filled with bitterness and scorn,
And shrivelled inner graces exposed this sharp-edged thorn.
Such seeds only bear strangled trees with fruit that offends,
Whose poisons weakened all those she touched and once called friends.
Her pain clouded God's provision for faith to believe
Vindication for her honour, His own plan would weave.

What would bring true release, purpose and joyful living?
Only God's Word could penetrate, heal and bring singing.
But the precious gift, for which she prayed and begged, could not.
So grief turned to anger, becoming an ugly blot.
However, love's rebuke, at last, helped her understand,
That better than ten sons was her husband's love so grand!

Realizing the great love-gift that was still hers, she bowed,
Now before God, transformed in her heart and mind she vowed,
As a fragrant sacrifice—giving up all desire—
No longer hers to own, His true love could now inspire;
"Over to You, dear Lord, Yours to keep, to use, to bless,"
Confessing sorrow for sin, "remove my selfishness."

Out of the depths of her lessons from sorrow and trial
Would come a great servant through whom God would reconcile,
To Israel, a leader, a great judge for their dark hour.
After years of silence God would speak now in power.
That child? That man born from worship and grace to excel?
God's answer for His people—Hannah's boy, Samuel!

Is my beloved Bridegroom asking of me the same?
Has my poor heart become swallowed up with grief untame?
Is there some consuming desire, stolen for my own?
Just guilt, defeat and only worthless days have I known?
Now, what will it take to break my self-inflicted pain,
That He, as Lord and Saviour, be lifted up again?

When God reaches deep within, to form and mould my way,
Yet sharp goads, like sin, remain in the heart of life's clay,
Though our Potter spins the wheel, working life in the marred,
All my jagged points shred His hands, already so scarred!
"O Lord, forgive my sin, because of Calvary's Hill.
How could I have chosen things that only wound and kill?"

"So, like Hannah, Lord, may I surrender before Thee,
To accept willingly Thy Will and Plan completely.
To be Your handmaid, a servant in whom You delight,
How I pray that all my desire will with Yours unite—
For You must have first place, our Greater than Samuel,
Because Your **Love Gift** to us—
                              **Is our Emmanuel!"**

*For the word of God  
is living and active.  
Sharper than any double-edged sword,  
it penetrates even to dividing soul  
and spirit, joints and marrow;  
it judges the thoughts  
and attitudes of the heart.*

(Hebrews 4:12 NIV)

"Our own words are mere paper pellets  
compared with the rifle shot of The Word."

Charles Haddon Spurgeon  
The Greatest Fight in the World  
Final Manifesto, p. 24.

# Ministering Life

Why is it we are helped when many preachers speak?
Others say the same words but leave us feeling weak.
Not just the possession of some powerful gift
That manifests itself or appears to uplift
But, also the heart's inward work and depth of grace—
Are we the thing we speak, a mirror of His face?

The difference?—The heart itself without dispute.
What we are before God, there is no substitute.
As the Lord becomes more and more our sustenance,
Things, even gifts, attach less and less importance.
Understanding creeds and knowing God, Adonai,
Two different things, such truth we cannot deny.

Though we may teach the same holy doctrine divine
How they are lived still reveals a dividing line.
One impacts hearts and lives with proving evidence,
While the other lacks life and sinful consequence.
The Spirit's work? Yes—His loving hand holds the knife.
Clearly, our power source for "ministering Life!"

*"How often do we attempt work for God
to the limit of our incompetency
rather than to the limit of
God's Omnipotency?"*

Hudson Taylor

Taken from *Goforth of China*, Rosalind Goforth, © 1925, p. 102.

# Lessons Simply Painted, Not Spoken!

"Precious Fellowship"
Favourite Forest-Beaverton Estate

How precious...are thy thy thoughts unto me,
O God!

(Psalm 139:17)

# Lessons Simply Painted, Not Spoken!

### *Original storyline idea: Source unknown*

A great preacher shared this simple story,
One penetrating precept for God's glory.
Into a great hall some men were all led
To learn wisdom for the days just ahead.
All who use this Truth and all it imparts
Will receive real comfort and strengthened hearts.

Sets of paintings were hung by careful choice,
Duplicates by visions, but not in voice.
At first glance the vistas seemed the same,
Yet, some were like arrows spent without aim.
Like shade without pleasure, days without light!
What was the answer? Had sense taken flight?

Those pictures sparkled like lighthouse towers,
But these—lifeless, like stems without flowers!
Yet the old Master artist would conclude
With the answers for the questions pursued—
The reasons why feeling and thoughts would soar—
To encourage trust in God all the more.

Creatures, like choirs, sang anthems and praised
As stately trees swayed with their branches raised.
By perfumed gardens and falls that cascade
One could almost feel the cool of their shade!
Yes, rich havens for peace, worship and prayer
Ministering grace and God's loving care.

But how was life shared and senses stirred,
Or God's "still small voice," in love, clearly heard?
What was this tool that made the difference,
Transforming their hearts with such influence?
His reply, a profound but simple truth,
That we should have learned from our early youth.

Why was every heart so touched or broken
By lessons simply painted, not spoken?
The answer, like shafts, shot straight from God's bow
Where you find depth to life, you find Shadow!
"Jewels," hidden in burdens of measure,
Though from darkened depths, now become Treasure!

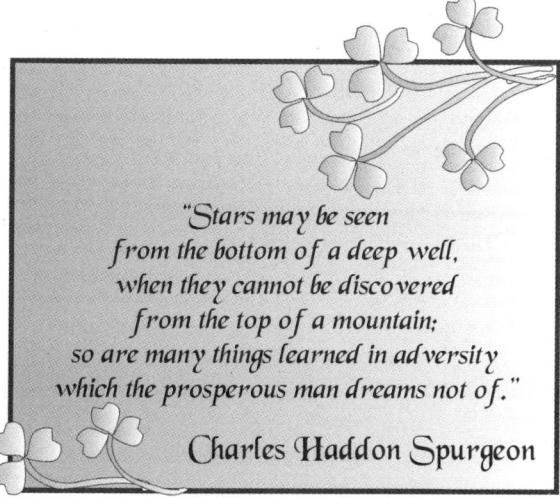

"Stars may be seen from the bottom of a deep well, when they cannot be discovered from the top of a mountain; so are many things learned in adversity which the prosperous man dreams not of."

Charles Haddon Spurgeon

Taken from *Goforth of China*, Rosalind Goforth, © 1937, p. 210.

The angel of the LORD encampeth round about them that fear him and delivereth them. O taste and see that the LORD is good: blessed is the man that trusteth in him.

(Psalm 34:7,8)

# Silent Sufferings

As God's servants live through conflict and that which seems a waste,
In trouble or distress we are tempted to act with haste.
We feel almost ruined, abused by those who jeer and taunt—
If only we had support of a friend or confidant,
Just one with whom our burdened sufferings we could share;
But God understands why we must remain alone in prayer.

So, with questioning heart I ask if God is checking sin—
I interrogate my soul, question and cross-examine.
Even then, it seems I hardly know my inner spirit
Can I let such silence teach me peace though others fear it?
"Yes dear Lord, even if it includes this long dark moment."
Yet it still seems like an endless nightmare, an infringement.

"Father You know I am very fragile, as well as frail,
And how much secret battering I can stand and not fail.
Lord, long before I cry out You design and utilize
Plans for my good—even though just now it seems otherwise."
Yes, it is a special process we've been called to pass through
Where faith becomes fact, and deep trust transforms and strengthens you.

Since we must know first hand the grace of dwelling in His courts,
He will grant earthly solace with gifts of special comforts.
For we are not alone; Yes, His servants still watch and pray
Sympathizing with us, showing God's love to us today.
At the right moment His healing balm at last overflows
He comforted them in their hour, now they can share our woes!

*Praise...the God of all comfort,*
*who comforts us in all our troubles,*
*so that we can comfort those in any trouble*
*with the comfort we ourselves have received from God.*
*For just as the sufferings of Christ flow over into our lives,*
*so also through Christ our comfort overflows.*

(2 Corinthians 1:3-5 NIV)

*Consider it pure joy, my brothers,
whenever you face trials of many kinds,
because you know that the testing
of your faith develops perseverance.
Perseverance must finish its work so
that you may be mature and complete,
not lacking anything.*

(James 1: 2-4 NIV)

"*If a potter does not bring his clay to maturity slowly
it would be impotent. So...the potter
imposes certain conditions on his clay
not to constrict it but to support it,
not to enfeeble it but to empower it.*"

Nell Kennedy

Taken from Worthy Vessels, Nell Kennedy, Zondervan Books, ©1985, p. 65.
Used by permission of Nell Kennedy.

# Patience And Desert Honey!

My son, keep my words,
And treasure my commandments within you.
Keep my commandments and live,
And my teaching as the apple of your eye.

(Proverbs 7: 1-2 NASB)

# Patience And Desert Honey!
## The Hard Lesson of Waiting Patiently

I think one of the more difficult lessons to learn in life is the willingness to *wait patiently* for God's timing. Indeed, it is especially hard to learn this lesson when we are in a big rush for immediate help or direction for life. We want those solutions now, not sometime tomorrow or months into the future.

In effect, we snap our prayer fingers and expect to be instantly gratified with the needed action from God that will bring our request into being. But, in all fairness, many times we do so because we sincerely believe with all of our heart that what we ask for is clearly God's Will. And, in such instances, *patience* does not seem to be warranted. However, when those answers are delayed, it can become confusing and very distressing, and may severely test the elasticity of our faith.

Sometimes, during long spans of silence and pause, it may make the journey of *waiting* seem more like we are living in the middle of a burning desert than in a pleasing oasis of obedience to the Saviour. Somehow the reward of such obedience is veiled.

Often it is not until we are able to look back on a situation that we see God's Divine plan operating. If we do not have complete understanding, then at least we can know that there was eternal purpose assigned to those painful delays. It is after we have submitted to His Will to *wait*, whether willingly or forced, that we have also found amazing evidence that our Sovereign Lord was, after all, in complete control. He was orchestrating only that which would bring ultimate blessing and peace into our lives. At the same time, as His Will was wonderfully accomplished, God was glorified in our lives.

As we know, even the children of Israel soon discovered that their Redeemer was right there with them in their desert travels: sustaining them, directing their steps and yes, lovingly carrying them through every sandstorm, every scorching element and every dark hour of loneliness. He was transforming their hearts as He cared for them like a loving Shepherd—like a Shepherd Who carries a wounded lamb into the fold to safety after darkness falls.

As pure gold is transformed in the fire, so are God's children. The fiery process goes on until we reflect the glory of our beloved Saviour: A process that cannot be rushed or completed by taking shortcuts. I was learning these same lessons as I studied an illustration on how the Bedouins produced palm-honey. It's compelling truth led me to write about the spiritual necessity of *waiting* and trusting God's perfect plan. I needed to patiently allow the Lord to bring forth His precious fruit, in His own way, through my life—fruit that will last for all Eternity.

# Patience And Desert Honey!

Yes, in some parts of the Sinai Desert wasteland
Bedouins gather palm-tree honey yet by hand.
And safe into cloth sacks—woven of sheer-like wool—
Hang them from tree branches to form a crucible.
The honey is left to drip *slowly* into urns,
Often taking days to ooze forth, to gain returns!

When one young man tried to rush this weary process,
He compressed the cloth with impatient eagerness.
But, an old woman waved gnarled fingers in his face,
And, from behind her veil, scolded him with disgrace.
"My Son!—To touch the bag is to streak the honey;
To streak the honey lessens it's worth for money!"

Just as with *desert honey* so with *desert Truths*,
They can't be rushed like life in Egypt's tents or booths.
But, through the filters of such crucibles of fire
Our faith extracts rich treasures, free from filth and mire—
Impurities now caught in these chambers of cloth:
Those unholy leavens that only spoil and froth.

All too often we cannot hear God on the run,
As we live busy lives or work to serve God's Son.
But, like Elijah in the quiet of God's Mount,
Or Moses by the rock or Mara's bitter fount,
So too, we come to know—apart on bended knee—
Only *quiet patience*—

Gives us **desert honey!**

*Rest in the LORD, and wait patiently for him.*
*(Psalm 37:7)*

*For there is one God
and one mediator
between God and men,
the man Christ Jesus,
who gave himself as a ransom for all.*

(1 Timothy 2:5,6 NIV)

"An expert swimmer states,
'A drowning man cannot be saved
until he is utterly exhausted
and ceases to make the slightest effort
to save himself.'"

Watchman Nee

Taken from *The Normal Christian Life*, Watchman Nee,
Victory Press © 1957, p. 117.

# Safe Ice?

The Trent Waterways, Ontario, Canada

*Trust in the LORD with all thine heart; and lean not unto thine own understanding.*

(Proverbs 3:5)

*Let not your heart be troubled, neither let it be afraid.*

(John 14:27)

# The Story Behind "Safe Ice?"
## Missionaries home on furlough...

It was an exciting morning for the church congregation. Anticipation ran high as the missionary stepped up to the microphone. Gerald and his little family had just arrived home safely from Cote D'ivoire, West Africa, after years of dedicated service.

We knew that they would have much to share with us over the next hour, and we in turn would have much for which to praise the Lord. We were not disappointed.

But the report also brought each of us a challenge of the heart and a new need for prayer as the missionary humbly shared how he was facing a new and unexpected direction in his life—one that, if looked upon in the flesh, could become overwhelming and a cause for dreading the unknown.

Gerald spoke of an amazing responsibility that was so far beyond his experience, capabilities or even his desire. Added to this was the fact that there was so little time for him to learn how to accomplish the task now set before him. Yet, Gerald also spoke of the clear and undeniable leading of his Lord in the matter.

He was honest in confessing that he was standing before us in fear and trembling. But he also spoke with a sense that he clearly knew that no matter what lay ahead of him he could trust his Saviour to lead, to enable him to obey and to do the impossible.

He used a vivid illustration to demonstrate how he was feeling. He described a team of strong workhorses pulling a sleigh filled with carefree passengers. Racing over a snow bank and down a steep hill at top speed, they headed straight toward a frozen pond. He imagined his thoughts if he were on board, not knowing if the ice would hold their weight or give way, or if they would all crash through the surface!

As I listened I was struck by God's message to my own heart through this dear brother in the Lord. All I could think about for the rest of the day was the haunting question of **trust**. Would I trust the Lord even when my circumstances seemed life threatening, overwhelming and completely out of my control? Or, would I shrink from the task?

As I wrestled with those thoughts I also knew that, for the moment, all I really needed to do was to obey the clear leading that Christ had *already* given to me. That was not in question.

So I chose to surrender my doubts and fears and rest in God's arms: in His Strength, in His Wisdom, in His Love and in His so great Salvation.

As a result, putting my own twist to it, I wrote "Safe Ice?" to remind myself of the lesson I had just learned...

# "Safe Ice?"

Many years ago, it is told now by some,
One earnestly prayed his fears to overcome.
Gingerly, by the edge of some pond of ice
Placed his foot on that cold, frosty, flat device.
*"Safe Ice?"* Yes, the signpost had clearly stated,
Yet doubts marred his trust and left faith frustrated.

While the forest breathed peace and scents of green pine,
Winter's air bristled, chilling deep to the spine;
The ice moaned, cracked, and curls of steam filled the air,
Still he anxiously prayed, "Lord, please lift my care."
So his fears eased, and as his courage renewed
He tried to move, yet to that spot he stayed glued!

By faith his other foot he should be lifting,
But he faltered when his weight started shifting.
Suddenly, he heard a strange, thunderous sound
As snow billowed up like a cloud from the ground—
There where earth's edge and sky meet just at the rim,
At the top of the hill—just in front of him!

But before the sights and sounds came together
A heavy sled, couched with joy bells and leather
Pulled by four teams of strong, magnificent mounts—
With no notice for advancing speeds or counts—
"Swoosh"—Just like the speed of light, to be precise!
They headed straight for this very pond of ice!

His heart pounding—his brow cold, beaded with sweat—
Would the ice hold? Could they keep from getting wet?
The sled weighed a ton, and the horses much more,
But the folks on board laughed in a joyous roar.
They knew the sign, **"Safe Ice,"** meant just what it said;
No need to worry now—just follow that sled!

Right over that pond, in the blink of an eye
Across in safety—they just flew right on by!
But why, then, was he still staring at that sign?
*"Safe Ice?"* Would he shift his weight over that line?
Would he faithfully it's promise demonstrate?
**If God said, "Safe Ice,"—**
                    **Would he still hesitate?**

*Let not your heart be troubled: ye believe in God,
believe also in me.*

*Jesus saith unto him, I am the way, the truth, and the life:
no man cometh unto the Father, but by me.*

*If ye love me, keep my commandments.*

*At that day ye shall know that I am in my Father,
and ye in me, and I in you.*

*He that hath my commandments, and keepeth them,
he it is that loveth me:
and he that loveth me shall be loved of my Father,
and I will love him, and will manifest myself to him.*

(John 14:1,6,15,20-21)

*"Each of us may be sure that if God
sends us on stony paths,
He will provide strong shoes.
He will not send us out on any journey
for which He does not equip us well."*

**Megiddo Message**

Taken from Flowers Along The Path, Esther Carls Dodgen,
Barbour Publishing, © 2001, p. 242. Used by permission.

*"Fear not tomorrow,
for God is all ready there."*

Author Unknown

1 "Glorious Journey"

Jesus saith unto him,
I am the way, the truth, and the life:
no man cometh unto the Father, but by me.

(John 14:6)

2

³ "Commitment"

As for me and my house,
we will serve the LORD.

(Joshua 24:15)

"Little Willy"

### 4 "Invitation to Worship"

Come, let us bow down in worship,
let us kneel before the LORD our Maker;
for he is our God and we are
the people of his pasture,
the flock under his care.

(Psalm 95:6,7 NIV)

### 5 "God's Love"

God has given us eternal life, and this life is in his Son [Jesus Christ].

(1 John 5:11 NIV)

6 "Glorious Resurrection"
Hebrews 13:5

For He [God] Himself has said,
I will not in any way fail you nor give you up
nor leave you without support.
[I will] not, [I will] not, [I will] not in any degree
leave you helpless nor forsake nor let [you] down
(relax My hold on you)! [Assuredly not!]

(Hebrews 13:5 AMP)

7

8 "God's Cleansing Power"

Create in me a pure heart, O God...

(Psalm 51:10 NIV)

9 "Winged Treasures"

10 "The Old Road Home"

Thou wilt shew me the path of life:
in thy presence is fulness of joy...

(Psalm 16:11)

11 "Favourite Forest-Precious Fellowship"

## 12 "Apples of Truth"

My son, keep my words
And treasure my commandments...and live,
And my teaching as the apple of your eye.

(Proverbs 7:1,2 NASB)

# Proving Grounds

*Thy shoes shall be iron and brass; and as thy days, so shall thy strength be.*

(Deuteronomy 33:25)

*Lacy's First Prize - Country Fair*

*Not that I have already obtained all this, or have already been made perfect, but I press on to take hold of that for which Christ Jesus took hold of me.*

*I press on toward the goal to win the prize for which God has called me heavenward in Christ Jesus.*

(Philippians 3:12-14 NIV)

# Proving Grounds

## "Where the bitter becomes the sweet."

As I wrote the poem "Proving Grounds," I was thinking of my own past desert places and circumstances that had been filled with scorching trials. But as I looked back, each one had become a fertile "proving ground."

Yet proving grounds can, for a time, become stark and appear to be hopeless places. If some of those painful places are filled with unresolved sufferings, questions and fierce spiritual battles, they may crowd us into very dark corners.

If I am forced to remain in those unwanted corners allowing my doubts to fester unchecked, I may begin to think, by His apparent silence, that the Lord has abandoned me. If, to my mind, my questions remain with inadequate answers, injured trust can deteriorate into unbelief, anger or even deep disillusionment.

I think most of us have knowledge of such places. When we find ourselves unable to understand what is happening to us, or perhaps what is *not* happening to us, then our hope may also degenerate into an empty and numbed resignation.

Enduring these long ongoing battles without direct answers to unceasing prayers—prayers in which we beg God to make His Will evident or to show us what to do next—may also cause us to lose heart and give up emotionally. But the potential for this kind of emotional defeat shocks and frightens us, and because we can only see the seeming impossibility of a situation, battle fatigue deepens even further.

If disappointment sets in, instead of the expected infusion of needed life and the strengthening of an undaunted faith, just the opposite effect seems to be taking place. Although we long for rescue as well as purpose in our suffering, it seems as if our faith will not survive this terrible testing.

We envision the enemy circling overhead, like a demon vulture, just waiting for the celebration of the death of yet another defeated, useless Christian. And with each new victim, it seems God Himself is ultimately being defeated also. But this is not so. Far from it! In spite of how we may feel or how things may *appear* outwardly, Jesus Christ continues to be *"the same yesterday and today and forever"* (Hebrews 13:8, NIV).

Our heavenly Father holds us secure. Sometimes, when we face such circumstances, we may need to realize afresh that we have nothing else left to hold on to and finally throw ourselves into God's arms. We abandon our will into His Will, because we have truly come to the end of ourselves.

Although we still have no strength of our own, in that precious moment, when we cease to struggle, we can truly rest from spiritual, emotional and even physical exhaustion.

As we do so, we also find that this is exactly when the Saviour swoops in like a great eagle to catch her falling chicks in mid-flight, to carry them to safety. So too, we learn that God carries us in His arms, safely into victory and out of every dark corner.

How comforting and reassuring to realize, afresh, that God knows exactly how much we can endure. Indeed, many times these solitary places become precious places of refuge, protection and unexpected entranceways that clearly lead us in a new direction, but a direction that leads away from further dangers and unthinkable disasters.

What love and mercy we would have missed had we not sojourned in this "proving ground," a proving ground where the bitter becomes the sweet, and where surrender is complete. We are exactly where we belong now. This is the place we can call home— because we are resting in the arms of our Lord and Saviour, Jesus Christ. And if we are resting in His arms we are in the Secret Place, whether here on earth or in Glory, and we are forever safe.

# Proving Grounds

Proving grounds can seem so like a wilderness
As unanswered questions fill me with distress;
My will lays prostrate on that parched, desert crust,
Where faith seems choked in mountains of ash and dust.

Demon vultures, starved and gaunt, buzz overhead
For a banquet, since faith seems as good as dead.
But God knows how much our frail frames can now stand
By this better way, south, through this desert land.

He spares us the unthinkable of the North.
Praise God His faithfulness will soon bring us forth.
But in this wasteland God makes the bitter sweet—
If my whole heart and life I lay at His feet!

*Open thou mine eyes, that I may behold
wondrous things out of thy law.*

(Psalm 119:18)

> "Faith discerns even behind the
> Beast the hand of God—
> for second causes make good disguises
> and baffle any eye
> but the eye of faith."
>
> Arthur Miller, Missionary

Taken from *Green Leaf in Drought-Time*, Isobel Kuhn, OMF International © 1957 p. 81. Used by permission.

> "The promise 'nothing shall be impossible to you' is conditional,
> valid only within the framework of God's will.
> Mountain moving faith is not faith in oneself,
> much less faith in faith, but faith in God.
> It is not faith itself, no matter how great,
> that moves mountains, but the God in whom the faith is grounded.
> Faith has only as much power as its object."

John MacArthur
(on Matthew 17:14-21)

Taken from *The MacArthur New Testament Commentary: Matthew 16-23*, by John MacArthur, Moody Publishers © 1988, p. 81. Used by permission.

> Let the words of my mouth,
> and the meditation of my heart,
> be acceptable in thy sight, O LORD,
> my strength, and my redeemer.
>
> (Psalm 19:14)

> "Faith gathers the handfuls of sacred corn
> from which contemplation threshes out the ears
> and prepares soul-sustaining bread."
>
> Haddon Spurgeon
> *The Best of C. Haddon Spurgeon, p. 38.*

> "Love to God will induce meditation.
> Neglect of meditation argues want of love."
>
> C. Haddon Spurgeon
> *The Treasury of David, Vol.3, p. 443, Psalm 119:97.*

# Loved

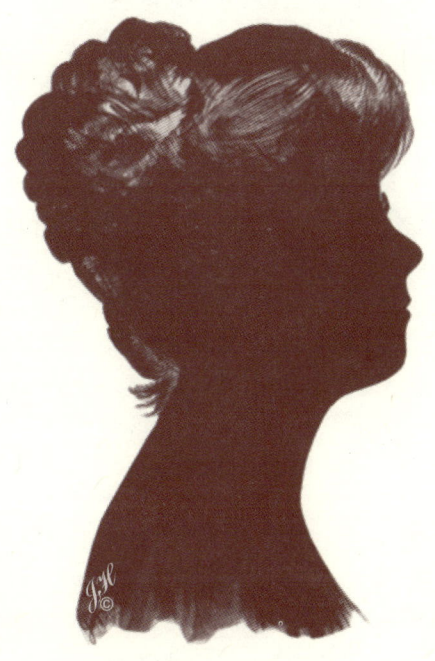

Thou wilt shew me the path of life:
in thy presence is fulness of joy;
at thy right hand there are pleasures for evermore.

(Psalm 16:11)

## Loved By One Who Loves God!

Now not every housewife in this day and age
Can boast that her marriage is a rich, full wage.
Having one special man to cherish, to love,
Honour with reverence with God's love from above—
So first my submission is to our Lord God,
Then to my spouse, my friend; I praise, I applaud
Because I am still loved by one who loves God!

There is much inner love I wish I could say
With powerful words to express the deep way
I've come to love you. Truly in a real sense
Who you are and will yet become, in essence,
Is to grow in likeness of God's own loved Son.
Thanks I give to Him for you and all He's done.
We are His; I am yours; still one in His Son.

How precious to be safe in the Father's Will,
Knowing He is Sovereign and faithful still.
We walk day by day, step by step, two as one—
All these years, His faithfulness our trust has won.
So we together, as long as we both live,
Can, by God's great grace, share and joyfully give
His Word, His Music: so other lambs too shall live!

*Happy 15th Wedding Anniversary*
*For my precious Ross. August 26, 1987.*

*Lovingly, Your Janny xoxox*

"The things that make God dear to us
are not as much His great big blessings
as the tiny things; because they show
His amazing intimacy with us;
He knows every detail of our individual lives."

Oswald Chambers

Taken from *Green Leaf in Drought-Time*, Isobel Kuhn,
OMF International, © 1957, p. 111. Used by permission.

Because thy lovingkindness is better than life,
my lips shall praise thee.
Because thou hast been my help, therefore in
the shadow of thy wings will I rejoice.

(Psalm 63:3,7)

"What to our eyes is a very pit of darkness
is to those children of His love
only the shadow of His wings!"

Amy Carmichael

Taken from *Gold By Moonlight*, Amy Carmichael, Christian Literature
Crusade, © 1935, p. 35. Used by permission.

## Love's Treasure

### Dear Dan,

Once upon a time there were two little tykes,
One little boy and girl, very much alike;
Yes, they could so easily have passed for twins
As they toddled hand in hand, all smiles and grins.

But now it was just a spoken remembrance,
That day—their last of any significance—
You see, war years made life difficult and drained;
This story of lost love was all that remained.

That young mother's turmoil, with so much at stake,
Overwhelmed her with the choices she must make.
Of course, this altered plans for those little lives—
Now three hearts suffered—wounded by many knives.

This pushed them in two different directions
Although they would have love and kind affections,
But raised together—to share life in measure?
No—They would mature, but not with that treasure.

A gentle man now, with resolve and backbone;
Married, with a sweet boy and girl of his own.
But all through those years, innocent of one truth—
That he had a sister, displaced since their youth.

Then one day a strange letter was delivered;
As he read the words *your sister* he shivered!
Could this be real? Just his imagination?
But, all he read brought tears for celebration!

It was true! He had a sister all his own!
No second thoughts, he called her by telephone.
The voice she heard took her by complete surprise;
She could not speak or her tears of joy disguise.

It was such a wonderful conversation,
To at last share their love and consolation.
Yes, God had answered the long decades of prayer,
Granting sweet reunion and their need to share!

On this momentous day—for this girl and boy—
Words could not hardly describe their nervous joy,
How they felt, what it meant and now the glory
It would bring God, the Author of their story!

For their first hellos, shyly they hugged and kissed,
Both had big dark-brown eyes, which no one had missed—
Searching those eyes was like facing a mirror
Brother and sister? Nothing could be clearer!

But, who were these two children in our story?
Once just secrets over which to feel sorry?
The little boy? Their mother's first-born son, Dan,
The young girl who prayed—was me,

*Your Sister, Jan!*

*Even so it is not the will of your Father which is in heaven, that one of these little ones should perish.*

*(Matthew 18:14)*

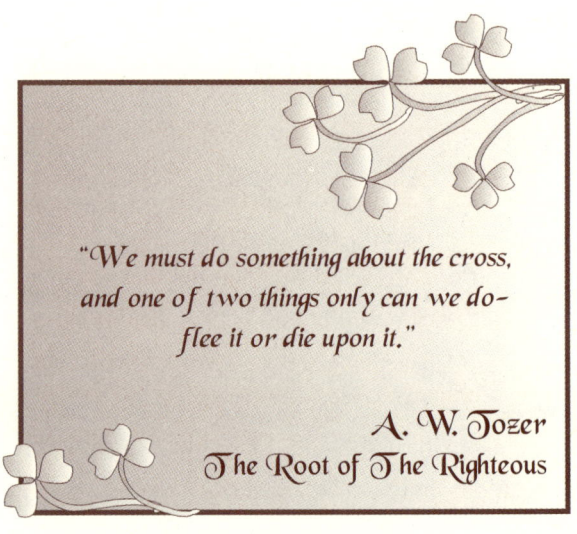

"We must do something about the cross, and one of two things only can we do— flee it or die upon it."

A. W. Tozer
The Root of The Righteous

Taken from *The Best of Tozer*, Compiled by Warren Wiersbe, by Christian Publications Inc., © 1978, p. 133. Used by permission.

"Only clay that is flexible and adaptable ever achieves its true identity."

Nell Kennedy

Taken from *Worthy Vessels*, Nell Kennedy, Zondervan Books, ©1985, p. 44. Used by permission of Nell Kennedy.

But thanks be to God,
who always leads us in triumphal procession
in Christ and through us spreads everywhere
the fragrance of the knowledge of him.
For we are to God the aroma of Christ
among those who are being saved
and those who are perishing.
To the one we are the smell of death; to
the other, the fragrance of life.

(2 Corinthians 2:14-16 NIV)

"There are times in life when the one place
in all the world where we can find
what we are seeking is the
Garden of Gethsemane."

Amy Carmichael

Taken from *Gold By Moonlight*,
Christian Literature Crusade, © 1935, p. 50. Used by permission.

# Birthday Cards Sent From God!

"Glorious Resurrection"

For He [God] Himself has said,
I will not in any way fail you nor give you up
nor leave you without support.
[I will] not, [I will] not, [I will] not in any degree
leave you helpless nor forsake nor let [you] down
(relax My hold on you)! [Assuredly not!]
(Hebrews 13:5 AMP)

# "Birthday Cards Sent From God!"
## Lifetime Friend

Besides browsing in libraries, fabric stores, flower and gift shops, writing devotionals or painting my watercolours, one of my favourite things to do is to spend time looking at all the wonderful greeting cards in card shops or in the card aisle in my grocery store on shopping day!

And that's what I was doing when all of a sudden my eye was captured by a colourful and elegant card. In flowing gold script it read, "For My Lifetime Friend!" I almost said right out loud, "That card is for Ruth!"

Ruth Ball and I became fast friends some thirty-three years ago while on a camping trip with two other girls. Ruth now lives in Texas, but we are still very close. We think alike in so many ways and share the Lord in a precious fellowship. Our hearts were knit together by the Lord.

As I picked up the card and read the words inside, they were very moving, and they imbedded themselves into my heart. Unfortunately the card turned out to be a birthday greeting. Now I hesitated—disappointed because I didn't think it was her birthday. Yet, the longer I thought about it and how the Lord sometimes asks the unusual of us, the more it didn't seem to matter. I felt constrained to send it to her anyway! So what if it looked foolish or strange? All I knew was that the message was beautiful and so truly custom tailored for my dear friend Ruth that I could not ignore it.

I put it on the kitchen table, and each day I asked the Lord to guide me as to when I should mail it. Though we are very close, for some odd reason throughout all our years of friendship we had never exchanged birthday cards. You can understand then why I was unsure at first, because I had absolutely no idea when her day really was! Nevertheless, I prayed that if it was important for it to arrive on her actual birthday that God would cause that to happen.

A week and half later, all of a sudden, I felt very burdened to mail the card that very day, without delay! Seven days later, I received a message on our answering service from Ruth. She had been deeply touched and encouraged by the card. She could barely describe how timely the need was for her to be girded up with God's love—the kind of love found in that card! She had been through many dark storms in the last weeks: distressing events, poor health, including unexpected eye problems that threatened a detached retina. Moreover, in the midst of all this turmoil, adding insult to injury, she had received unwarranted verbal abuse as well.

Needless to say, Ruth was feeling somewhat defeated and very down-hearted when the card arrived. But, it was just what she needed!

Certainly, it would be very easy to feel that nobody cared and that maybe even God had forgotten her. But, just when those feelings were rising—bang! There was a shower of love directly from the Lord Himself! Isn't that a special encouragement for our hearts as well? To think that when we as Christians are sensitive to the leading of the Holy Spirit, even in seemingly misguided, silly or senseless gestures, they can end up becoming God's vehicle to minister to those in great need! A simple task with a profound purpose in the hands of Almighty God.

It is also incredible to think that you and I can become God's paintbrush on the canvas of someone else's life and, with just a few strokes, become instruments of His Joy and Love, in spite of thousands of miles that may well separate us from them physically.

It is also a wonderful reminder of the unfathomable love and watch-care that our faithful God bestows on each of His children. He sees every hurt, every care and every burden that we carry. He will never leave us nor forsake us. That is His promise to us! So, if we too find ourselves aching and in deep need of being ministered to, remember God still sends us many unexpected tokens of His Love, at exactly the moment we so need them. And, sometimes God even sends us birthday cards! He may use an angel, or even a "lifetime friend." And when He does, we will know that there is no doubt that it was God who sent it!

"For [He [God] Himself has said,
I will not in any way fail you nor give you up
nor leave you without support.
[I will] not, [I will] not, [I will] not in any degree
leave you helpless nor forsake nor let [you] down
(relax My hold on you)! [Assuredly not!]"

(Hebrews 13:5 AMP)

# Birthday Cards Sent From God!
## *Lifetime Friend*

The food store was crowded and very busy·
As clerks worked at speeds that would make us dizzy.
Still the shoppers filled their carts full to the brim
While announcements told of old prices now trim.
Though tired and weary, I heard the clock chime
But I too was rushing, and quite pressed for time.

Yet, in spite of this great haste, still I made time
To find treasures and cards, in the five-and-dime.
There stood I gazing at all the best greetings—
Too many cards for my eyes were competing.
But wonderful respite and calm from the rush,
And just for a spell, the noise came to a hush!

Then all of a sudden this beautiful card
Wakened my senses like the perfume of nard.
A soft golden cord, braided in royal silk,
And deep kingly colours of green, beige and milk.
The elegant script and the precious dear words
"For My Lifetime Friend" just sang out like the birds.

But it sang its own song that beckoned my ears:
Not greetings of friendship or healing for tears,
But birth celebrations, and years long gone by—
Not what I looked for, but could not leave it lie:
Antique roses and wonderful words of truth
And I couldn't help think, this *must* be for Ruth!

Though, not her *birth* day, it would truly seem strange
Certainly Ruth will think this woman needs change!
The more I thought through in the God that I trust
It no longer mattered, now send it I must!
Gladly I bought it, and then straight home to prayer
Seeking God's lead when I should mail it by air.

Soon you will understand why I felt so torn
Because I had no clue when Ruth had been born.
But I knew God knew, and if truly needed
Blessings for my friend would not go unheeded.
So waiting for God, on His arm now I bent
And the chosen day when her card should be sent.

Days passed and I wondered, "Should I yet delay?"
But God's answer was strong, "No. Send it today!"
God in His great love chose the day it arrived
And news of surprise and true joy uncontrived
Brought tears filled with love, overflowing her cup
To think, God sent His Love just to gird her up!

The showers of Love were directly from Him
A card chosen with care and not on a whim.
Just to think that God's plan was to orchestrate
Each answer to prayer that we now celebrate;
Truly our God knew Ruth's need for assurance
And strength to trust Him, as well as endurance.

How glad to be used as a paintbrush for God,
By His Grace, instruments, though parted by sod—
You are precious; never forgotten by Him.
So was it your birthday by chance still so slim?
Now My Lifetime Friend says, no longer forlorn,
"It came March 6th,

*The very day I was born!"*

*He will not allow your foot to slip or to be moved;*
*He Who keeps you will not slumber...nor sleep.*

(Psalm 121:3,4 AMP)

The LORD is my strength
and song,
and he is become my salvation.

(Exodus 15:2)

"The Lord is near to all that call upon Him:
Yea, He can feel breath when no voice
can be heard for faintness."

John Trapp

# Alone, But God!
## Psalm 40:1-3

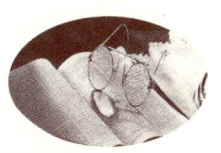

Precious souls quarantined in lonely, deathlike situations
Fear this dark word *alone*, picturing dreaded separations.
Fear that drives one's faith into exile when hope seems all but lost,
Detesting this heavy burden because it speaks now of cost.
Yes hopeless haunting symptoms, this kind of loneliness can bring,
As the heart cries within for ease from this weary, weary thing.

No—mere words cannot describe this kind of bitter wilderness
Where life suddenly shifts, bringing heartache and intense distress;
A place that reveals where we are and what we may yet become
When this kind of strain lingers from deep pain that grows burdensome.
If I start to blame and criticize, guilt multiplies those sins
When lost in self, I forget that Christ my victory still wins.

In those desperate hours I need a life-changing remedy!
But remembering His Love and care may not come easily—
Nor finding hearts able to honestly find praise in this thing
That has so completely emptied me of all reason to sing.
Nevertheless, God's cure begins with Scripture's command to praise,
In spite of the fact there just are no words left inside to raise!

But King David, The Psalmist, often overwhelmed and troubled
Was once trapped in a "slimy pit" like tar that churned and bubbled.
Alone—Abandoned—Yes, hunted and hated on every side
By those he had loved as dear friends now turned like Jekyll and Hyde!
Though cast down, he must trust and wait patiently in this dark place
Where he learned to cling to God's Salvation and unfailing grace!

Perhaps right now, or sometime in the future, you might just find
Yourself in this horrid "pit," *alone*, and waiting in the blind—
Chosen vessels, like Moses and like the bud on Aaron's rod—
So now the hymns of praise were put there, in David's mouth *by God!*
God would do for them what they could not do for themselves—alone,
And God will place, in us—
        new songs that fly straight—
                from Heaven's Throne!

*He [God] put a new song in my mouth, a hymn of praise to our God...*

(Psalm 40:3 NIV)

(1 Corinthians 10:13)

"If [God] plow, it is because He purposes a crop...The tests He sends or permits are in reality His vote of confidence, for He undertakes not to allow us to suffer any testing beyond our powers of endurance."

— Isobel Kuhn

Taken from *Green Leaf In Drought-Time*, Isobel Kuhn, OMF International, © 1957, p.7. Used by permission.

"Like the clay in the potter's kiln,
we are not merely strengthened by the
fiery trials of life—we are changed...
Let us not remember only hard times; but
let us expect beauty to come out of human suffering
even as loveliness comes from the potter's kiln."

— Nell Kennedy

Taken from *Worthy Vessels*, Nell Kennedy, Zondervan Books, © 1985, p. 122. Used by permission of Nell Kennedy

## Bent But Not Broken

In spite of fierce winter gales and deep crushing snows,
The Mountain Hemlock with striking beauty still grows.
Its needles are as delicate as the tall firs—
Dainty to the touch, and just as soft as feathers!

And yet, if we try to break its great bough, at length,
We will learn that deep therein lies its might and strength.
Though winds whip at it and the ground begins to shake;
Yes, it will bend and yield, but *no, it will not break!*

Neither bitter earthly storms, no matter how fierce,
Pull its strong roots from the ground nor its foothold pierce.
Though its form is bent low by the heavy snow floor,
It will straighten, proud and noble just like before!

So, if we be storm-tossed by harsh, trouble-bent winds
We need not crumble, though pressed by such disciplines.
For our strength, the Anchor who holds all of God's flock,
Is rooted and entwined in Christ, our Lord, our Rock!

Though afflicted in many ways but not now crushed;
Perplexed, but not without hope if silenced or hushed;
Persecuted, but not utterly forsaken;
Struck down? Perhaps, but not destroyed nor mistaken!

So, like the Apostle Paul, we do not lose heart,
And like Mountain Hemlocks, to us God's Truths impart;
The strength of Christ's Life is ours if we but partake—
When *we* must bend and yield, then—
                    *Neither will we break!*

*The LORD upholds all those who fall
and lifts up all who are bowed down.*

(*Psalm* 145:14 NIV)

## Ambush, Earthquakes and Blooming in the Dark!

It's easy to miss the things God may ordain
To use, to teach, to deepen and yes, sustain.
And, sometimes it is hard to see that God shares
Every hurt—Every pain, indeed *all* my cares:
Whether in loss of those I love and hold dear,
Needed things, or hopes of success and career.

If God's loving gifts come first wrapped in heartache,
Shaking life's ground once thought firm, like an earthquake—
Can I still see that God's sweet rescue may come
Through back doors of ambush, though I'm bruised and numb;
While others hurl straight toward me at full speed
To stir up my heart to some very real need?

The Word of God's **truth** will stand through thick and thin,
And my trials are weighed and filtered now through Him.
When we suffer greatly through what seems unfair—
What to human hearts seems more than we can bear—
Still, through storms of faith, we pray—we yield—we bend.
Yes, in these sorrows let praise to God ascend.

Like Job, though stripped of all, yet still dependent,
Refused to sin, blame God or be irreverent.
And *if* our life is so bound and linked in God
Then *all* our heartaches become like "Aaron's Rod."
As we trust Christ in our storms, safe in God's Ark—
He will cause us to *bloom*—

### Right there in the dark!

*You are my lamp, O LORD;
The LORD turns my darkness into light.*
(2 Samuel 22:29 NIV)

*For you are precious to God.*

*In the shadow of his hand
hath he hid me, and
made me a polished shaft;
in his quiver hath he hid me.*

(Isaiah 49:2)

"Oh, shadowed, solitary ones,
remember how closely the
quiver is bound to the warrior,
within easy reach of the hand,
and guarded jealously."

Meyer
Christ in Isaiah

## Jesus Knows Every Teardrop

The Bible tells us in Psalm 56, verse 8
That God knows every tear we will accumulate.
Yes, into God's bottle each precious droplet falls,
Not one is lost or forgotten—each He recalls.
Not only that, please know, He has counted each one,
Recording them in His book as life's race is run.

What a loving Lord Who knows even when we cry,
Through our whole lifetime, to the moment when we die.
And, Jesus knows every hair we have on our head
Every deep desired prayer that we have cried or said.
He knows our troubles and the sins we try to hide
But forgives all, when we ask, with arms opened wide.

Jesus knows those things that burden our hearts with need,
Though we think God's forgotten or won't intercede.
Nothing escapes His attention, nor is He deaf—
When all is said and done, now there is nothing left;
Nothing to fear, to stop God or hinder His way—
Trust His Love, for He keeps us each and every day.

For He knew us before He formed us in the womb,
Before He made the world or flowers that would bloom.
He chose us then and made a way for us to live,
In Him by His great Salvation, and sin forgive.
So when we falter and our hearts fill up with fears,
Remember one day—
        Jesus will dry all our tears.

*Thou tellest my wanderings:*
*put thou my tears into thy bottle:*
*are they not in thy book?*

*(Psalm 56:8)*

# No More Mud Please!

One of the first lessons I had to learn as a watercolour artist was how to avoid making mud! However, the second lesson, which should probably have been the first lesson, was to learn the discipline of waiting for a passage of wet paint to become bone-dry before applying a new layer of colour over the first one.

The colours I chose also had to be correct. This is especially true when I use the *glazing method*. If I do not wait for each layer to dry, at best the only thing I will end up with will be dulled, lifeless pigments or unsightly water blooms that will spoil the overall effect of the piece. At worst, I will lose that lovely luminous glow because the dead, heavy colours will block out the treasured light of the white paper below. This will defeat the exquisite beauty and charm of using transparent watercolours. All I will have successfully created is what all artists dread, and that is *mud*!

Perhaps, like me, you sometimes find it difficult to wait for the Lord to put all the necessary layers into place that will cause His Will to become a reality in our lives. And when that process exceeds our time clock we become impatient thinking that He has forgotten us or that He has even abandoned us. When that happens, we may be tempted to take things into our own hands and begin to manipulate or twist plans and circumstances to fit what we either believe or hope is God's Will for us.

But choosing not to wait for the Lord's leading is a grave error in judgment, and will only bring bitter disappointment. Our effectiveness for His Kingdom will also be greatly reduced. Such choices will set us on a path that takes us backward instead of forward. And forward is where we wanted to be in the first place. Now those same decisions may lead us into territory that will cause deep confusion or circumstances that we may well come to regret.

If we do determine to take matters into our own hands, whether knowingly or not, it is not long until we realize in, no uncertain terms, that sadly we have marred the divine plan with the ugliness of our own sin. Clearly, when self gets in the way, we rob God of the praise He deserves for His leading and guiding in our lives.

The act of taking the controls, for even a short time, will only prove to be a snare to us and will hinder our fellowship with our dear Saviour.

That is a grief that is not worth any moment of selfish glory. We will find ourselves floundering in unnecessary turmoil and heartache: heartache that not only affects us personally but injures our loved ones as well. What we thought were such creative plans have only brought forth emptiness, and the only thing we have successfully created for ourselves in the process is spiritual *mud!*

Because glazing is one of the simple ways that a clean layer or veil of colour can be laid down upon another in a disciplined order, it will give the artist beautiful, luminous and glowing colours. This method allows the light to shine through each successive layer, which in turn reflects the glory of the colours below. This unique and expressive medium not only gives brilliancy and life but injects powerful emotions and impact into a picture.

The same principle is in operation when we allow our Heavenly Father to lead us and to fulfill His Will in our lives, in His timing. Then, like the light that shines through all the layers of the coloured pigments in my watercolour, so God's Love and Mercy can shine through every step of the journey and through every answered prayer for guidance. When it does, God receives all the Glory He so richly deserves!

Then one of the rewards we can enjoy is the deep satisfaction that we have obeyed by waiting for the Lord: that His perfect Will has, therefore, been accomplished in our lives.

As Psalm 91:14-16 reassures us, when we love God and choose to call upon Him, He will answer us. He will, in fact, deliver us and honour us in the process. When we continue in His Presence, in the Secret Place, there is no need to choose any other plan but His. "*His way is perfect…It is God that girdeth me with strength, and maketh my way perfect*"! (Psalm 18:30,32).

When we apply this biblical truth, we will have learned afresh how to avoid making *mud* in our lives! That is something not only artists meticulously seek after but, indeed, it is what every child of God knows is a worthy prize for which to strive. When it is found, it is a treasure to be cherished!

# Under His Tender Watch Care

"Invitation To Worship"

Come, let us bow down in worship,
let us kneel before the LORD our Maker;
for he is our God and we are
the people of his pasture,
the flock under his care.

(Psalm 95:6,7 NIV)

# Under His Tender Watch Care

I could barely see the body and form of our neighbour's cat through the misty morning light. He was huddled tight up against the trunk of the small tree that divided our backyards. From my upstairs window's vantage point, Willy did not look at all comfortable or happy.

I thought back to the previous day of high heat and humidity. Thankfully, by late evening a strong breeze had cooled the air dramatically. In fact, it was almost too damp and chilly to continue sitting on the back step with Willy.

Not only that, at the same time the June bugs were buzzing up at the windows and around our heads, disrupting our visit. I spent more time waving away the bugs than patting my little friend. Darkness was also setting in, and I soon realized Willy's owners were not returning from their day trip. For some reason, earlier in the day, Willy had missed the last call to get back into his house. I patted Willy and reluctantly sent him on his way. I knew he was in for another long, miserable night.

Only a few nights before, through no fault of his own, Willy had been left out overnight in a frightening electrical thunderstorm, with high winds travelling close to 90 kilometres an hour.

I felt sorry for this tender-hearted creature who so loved to be with people, safe in his own home or content on someone's lap.

As the lightning lit up the backyard and the rain came down in sheets, I remember seeing him that night, stiff with fear, cowering under a deck chair. Oh, how my heart ached seeing him in such distress, and I felt powerless to help him. At least tonight it was quiet.

I headed off to bed whispering a prayer to the Lord who sees every sparrow that falls (Matthew 10:29) and whom I knew would watch over little Willy as well.

Sometime during the pre-dawn hours I awakened, wondering if Willy was still outside. I peeked through the Venetian blinds. Sure enough there he sat, huddled under the tree waiting for any sign of life and for the golden opportunity to make his mad dash back into the house.

I thought to myself, "I'm sure he feels very alone, confused and abandoned. After all he is a house cat, not a wild cat." He was cold, hungry and anxious.

As this scene played over in my mind, I couldn't help think of a similar incident in the Bible. Christ's disciples, also, found themselves in a tremendous storm, alone, anxious and in desperate need of rescue.

The Lord had instructed them to take this journey alone. He would dismiss the great crowds and then spend some time in quiet. He needed to take time to pray on the mountainside: to be alone with His Father. Jesus promised to join them later.

It was a terrifying and vicious storm and the men were cold and stiff with exhaustion. Their questions may have included, "Where was the Saviour when we needed Him?" "Why did He not come with us?" "If only Jesus was in the boat, He would calm the storm." They may also have felt abandoned and very much alone as they fought to survive.

Certainly they *appeared* to be alone and in peril of perishing. But what they could not possibly know or see was that their Lord was, indeed, personally watching over them from the mountainside (Mark 6:48).

Jesus was well aware of the great storm that they were battling. He was literally with them *in* the storm, and would soon make that obvious to them. As they strained at the oars He knew just how much they could handle. He also knew the exact moment that He needed to step in to calm the storm, for their sakes, and rescue them. He knew how to use the storm to grow their faith.

But the picture that touched the core of my heart that morning was that of the uninterrupted *watch care* that God had for His own beloved disciples, as well as for you and me today. The great love that our Saviour showers upon each of us every day, taking us through every storm we must face, is amazing! Every moment that we must spend growing, by having to strain at the oars of our faith, if you like, helps us toward *"the mark for the prize of the high callng of God in Christ Jesus"* (Philippians 3:14).

On a miniature scale, I too was watching over Willy, though he did not know it or perceive it. I was praying on his behalf. And, if he had belonged to me, I could have scooped him up in my arms and rescued him at just the right moment.

As I thought about what I had seen from my window, I

climbed back into bed, but sleep eluded me. I couldn't protect Willy because he belonged to someone else, but God could and did. As my *lifetime friend* related to me, "God has put this little Willy, literally, right into your lap, to show you many spiritual lessons"—even treasures that come from abiding in the Saviour.

My heart was deeply comforted to realize afresh that because I belong to Jesus, if I find myself in a terrible storm, straining at the oars and feeling all alone, then I am not really alone at all! My Heavenly Father is watching over me, covering me with His wings and keeping me through every trial, safe in the Secret Place. He is All sufficient and All caring. I am truly blessed as I abide in my precious Saviour, Jesus Christ. God's Word is true:

## 15 "God's Strength"

*He who dwells in the shelter of the Most High will rest in the shadow of the Almighty. I will say of the LORD, "He is my refuge and my fortress, my God, in whom I trust."*

(Psalm 91:1,2 NIV)

*Thou wilt keep him in perfect peace,
whose mind is stayed on thee:
because he trusteth in thee.
Trust ye in the LORD for ever:
for in the LORD JEHOVAH is
everlasting strength.*

(Isaiah 26:3,4)

*You, O LORD, keep my lamp burning...
With your help I can advance against a troop;
with my God I can scale a wall.*

(Psalm 18:28,29 NIV)

# A Wall With No Door!

Sometimes, though I trust Christ as my Saviour and my Lord,
I face "roadblocks" I feel I can't handle or afford.
When I don't know exactly just what my Lord will choose
For the path upon which He will guide these earthly shoes—
Whether I may yet face some dark hedge or wall-like mass
Or that which might meet me on some hidden mountain pass.

Is there God's purpose for this complete and sudden halt
As I wonder, "Am I blameless; am I free from fault?"
Yet, there were no warning signs to change my direction—
Was not this very highway marked for my protection?
All the "sign posts" God gave, led **directly** to this spot
I prayed—He led—I followed. Then why this counterplot?

With no human means for escape—or continuing,
It seems as if, now, I'm at the end of everything.
So, I wait with quiet heart, my hand caught in His clasp,
As if all that I valued has fallen from my grasp!
And, I must weigh the fact God may plan to keep me here
For some lengthy time apart—or so it may appear.

My temptation is to help God and take the controls—
But struggles cannot be hurried or squeezed through loopholes.
For God is Sovereign and knows what He must now permit,
As this tunnel with no light is made to shape and fit.
But—I am surrounded—and this I cannot ignore
Because it's a concrete wall—but a *"wall" with no door!*

Still, it is by that *wall*, towering above me there,
I must continue trusting Jesus and rest in prayer.
Though feelings say, "God's forsaken me and will not keep,"
I know better, God neither slumbers nor will He sleep
The answer was in that wall, hidden deep at the core—
When I let Him use it—**then that wall**
                    **Became my door!**

# Silks of Ease

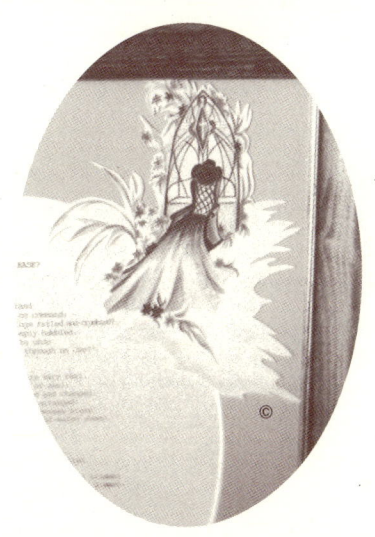

That you may live a life worthy
of the Lord and may please him in
every way: bearing fruit in every good work,
growing in the knowledge of God.

(Colossians 1:10 NIV)

## Silks of Ease

Just how do I begin to understand
Daily life that once played out on command?
I ask with shock, Lord, yet deeply humbled,
"Father, have those old things failed and crumbled?
Must safe routines I followed through on cue
Be exchanged now—yes, old plans for the new?"

Though battle zones for change are very real,
I tend to clutch at the old with great zeal.
As old frontiers are now challenged and changed,
Unrecognized, veiled and quite rearranged!
If webbed in silks of ease, my senses sleep,
And harsh winds may blow on this deaf-eared sheep.

But it seems easier to rest success
On keys tested by time and fruitfulness—
Yes, familiar ground, safe and comfort-filled
Remains, **if** storms are altogether stilled.
But, fruitful vines must still be pruned and trimmed,
Or their strength for growth will be lost or dimmed.

"Yet," struggle reasons, "Stop, don't go—Remain!
This strange new call *to go* cannot bring gain!"
But God knows just how to use to the full,
Your life, your gifts—If just available!
**Trust** God's Will and His **all-sufficiency**—
> **Yes, you are**
>> **God's Thread**—
>>> *For this tapestry!*

*Who shall separate us from the love of Christ?*
*shall tribulation, or distress, or persecution,*
*or famine, or nakedness, or peril, or sword?...*
*Nay, in all these things we are more*
*than conquerors through him that loved us.*
*For I am persuaded, that neither death,*
*nor life, nor angels, nor principalities, nor powers,*
*nor things present, nor things to come,*
*Nor height, nor depth, nor any other creature,*
*shall be able to separate us from the love of God,*
*which is in Christ Jesus our Lord.*

(Romans 8: 35-39)

"*The preparation of clay for service is*
*a long, slow process by which it gains*
*its unusual strength and resilience.*"

Nell Kennedy

Taken from *Worthy Vessels*, Nell Kennedy, Zondervan Books,
© 1985, p. 15. Used by permission of Nell Kennedy.

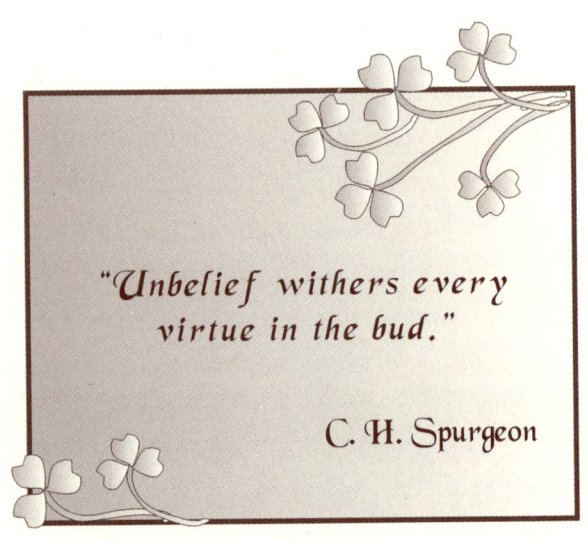

"Unbelief withers every virtue in the bud."

C. H. Spurgeon

Taken from *Gleanings Among the Sheaves*, by C. H. Spurgeon, Baker Books. Used by permission.

Just as you received Christ Jesus as Lord,
continue to live in him,
rooted and built up in him,
strengthened in the faith
as you were taught, and
overflowing with thankfulness.

(Colossians 2: 6,7 NIV)

# Shipwreck: Fickle Soft South Winds
## Acts 27:1-44

Wherefore, sirs, be of good cheer:
for I believe God, that it shall be
even as it was told me.

(Acts. 27:25)

# Shipwreck: Fickle Soft South Winds

There may be times when "soft south winds" will blow our way,
Which seem so plainly needed, yet may lead astray.
While they seem to guide and allow us to progress—
If misread can hinder God's plan for fruitfulness.

As I write to you, I'm safe and warm by my fire
Though chilly autumn storms whip at the old fence wire.
It's growing dark now, and lightning cracks and thunders
As night shadows cast out wispy, shaded wonders.

But, as damp drafts keep the porch shades gently swaying,
I drift to another storm and servants praying.
There aboard a Roman ship, caught in the late fall,
Chained with their prisoners? The great Apostle Paul!

His captors still debated about their next move,
Ignoring Paul's warning, which God would not approve.
"Winter in Fair Havens," Paul told the ship's master,
"You know fickle, soft south winds can bring disaster!"

The Roman guard thought this "south wind" was a sure sign
To sail on and accept what seemed to him divine.
Clearly, Paul declared that this grave error could cost
Precious lives and cargo; indeed, all might be lost!

Night after night they battled this wild hurricane,
And now the Apostle feared he too would be slain.
Just when all hope was gone, God's angel came to Paul
Promising him deliverance: Yes for them **all!**

Paul survived this shipwreck—and the storm retreated,
So God's plan for His servant would be completed.
Only the ship and goods were lost, just as Paul said,
Needless loss from signals they had clearly misread.

No matter how well such "signals" may seem to fit,
Push open doors of service for our benefit,
Don't run beyond God's perfect plan, or His Design—
***Wait*** for God's direction—
     and **Do His Will Divine.**

"Obedience is the one qualification for further vision."

G. Campbell Morgan

Taken from *Goforth of China*, Rosalind Goforth, © 1937, p. 51.

In all thy ways acknowledge him,
and he shall direct thy paths.

(Proverbs 3:6)

# Songbirds, Not Fighter Jets!

"Little Willy"

Peace I leave with you,
my peace I give unto you:
not as the world giveth, give I unto you.
Let not your heart be troubled,
neither let it be afraid.

(John 14:27)

## Songbirds, Not Fighter Jets!

Little Willy gladly curled up in a cozy ball on my lap, purring away contentedly. It had been a long, cold winter, but now we were both basking in the sunshine. As earlier storm clouds drifted away, the air was warming up; yet the atmosphere was still fresh and fragrant, and that sweetness drew out many beautiful songbirds, chirping and singing their hymns of praise to our Heavenly Father.

The gardens were filling with the lovely colours of crocus and tulips. The scent of lilac trees wafted by as the promise of new buds were forming on our Wygaleigh bush. As I relaxed, the effects of the strengthening moments of quiet with the Lord, and with Willy, washed over me. I breathed in the fresh air and raised my face upwards to the warmth of the sun's rays.

As I did so, I couldn't help notice that the heavens were unusually busy with all sorts of birds, large and small, zipping back and forth between the houses and the open backyards—some with definite purposes, while others were just playful, social skirmishes. Mrs. Robin was scolding one of her brood, and a small dog barked in the very far distance.

Indeed, it was fascinating to watch the birds dart in and out, flying freely from tree to tree, without once crashing into each other or into the buildings. They were wonderfully skilled, and their sense of distance was so precise that they never seemed to give it a second thought, but to my eyes it was God's amazing creation at work.

These little moments shared over a morning cup of tea on the back step were like mini vacations for me, and I was very grateful for these tranquil moments. But all of a sudden, that peacefulness was rudely interrupted by a loud bang, like a gun going off. The sound seemed to come from a distant building site. It startled both Willy and me.

Instantly I was reminded of the televised 2003 Iraq war, with the sound of bombs dropping out of war planes, exploding on their intended targets. Those sounds were fresh in my mind only because a few days earlier our quiet morning was suddenly shattered by the unnerving roar of a fighter jet screaming through our air space, literally just above our heads! Sighting a military jet is a very rare occurrence, in spite of the fact that Camp Borden is not far from where we live.

Consequently, in light of the age of *terror alerts*, concern and a chilling sense of danger instantly and boldly intruded on my peace of mind. Wondering why our solitude was being infringed upon, everyone raced to the window to see what was happening. I use the word *infringe* to describe this scene because the associated sound of that jet spoke of the need for protection, the warding off of evil intention and a need to restore peace.

Yet, as I sat on the step with Willy sleeping blissfully on my lap, the picture of birds busy at living life and playing with carefree abandon brought forth a flood of praise, because they were *just* birds and not fighter jets on a mission to kill and destroy invading enemies.

I shot up a prayer of thankfulness that the sounds in my ears were that of these musical songbirds and not, in fact, the roar of war planes warning of impending danger. How glad to know the quiet fluttering of their little wings were not plumes of smoke and that the loud bang I had heard earlier was not a massive bomb detonating.

Yes, I was grateful for the peacefulness of my morning with my dear little Willy. Even more than this momentary respite, I was all the more thankful for the indescribable gift of knowing God's Eternal peace in my heart because years earlier I had come to know His Son, the Prince of Peace, Jesus Christ, as my own personal Lord and Saviour.

This morning was an extra-special time for me with the Lord and His creation. He had used many beautiful songbirds to remind me of the peace and safety I have in Him, as I trust in His all-sufficient care and Salvation.

Yes, the roar of jets and the sense of danger may cause concern and real distress, but nothing can separate me from my Saviour, or the Peace that He is or the Peace that He alone provides (Romans 8: 38-39).

I said my goodbyes to little Willy and went back to face the day's work with a deep joy in my heart, knowing that no matter what I might face from day to day, my Saviour is my great Protector.

Now, every time I hear God's songbirds, I also remember my true treasure of Peace is Jesus.

# Sweet Little Willy!

Every morning and every afternoon,
Always beginning in the month of June,
Just like clockwork my furry little friend
Will sit alone, waiting for hours on end,
To hear the sound of the back door unlatch,
Knowing I'll melt, and my heart he will catch,
So at last he can just snuggle and nap—
Curled up like a ball, all warm in my lap.

Happy, cozy and safe, purring content,
Expecting this as an all-day event.
But there is so much work left yet to do
And I must still be on the move now, too.
He does not want me to go, but I must—
Protesting with paw, his tail in the dust—
Feigning to move, he starts then to get down,
But he climbs right back up; this little clown!

His antics I can't resist or ignore
And sometimes smother a laugh till I roar,
Or just huddle close when startled by jets
Calming thoughts, by talking away our frets.
Listening to God's songbirds to no end,
Here we sit—Just me and my little friend.
Grateful for the joy that Jesus imparts—
And His Peace that lives in my heart of hearts.

My loyal companion day after day—
How could I desert him and leave to play?
Will he survive without even a pat,
Or a tender, loving, squeeze by the mat?
Yes, he thinks I should also let him in
To stay for good—but nay, that would be sin.
You see, this friend does not live in my flat—
Sweet little Willy is my neighbour's cat!

*Let us throw off everything
that hinders and the sin
that so easily entangles,
and let us run with perseverance
the race marked out for us.
Let us fix our eyes on Jesus,
the author and perfecter of our faith.*

(Hebrews 12:1,2 NIV)

"True faith rests upon
the character of God and
asks no further proof than the
moral perfections of
the One who cannot lie."

A.W. Tozer,
*Man: The Dwelling Place of God*

Reprinted from *The Best of Tozer*, Compiled by Warren Wiersbe,
©1978 by Christian Publications, Inc., p. 169.
Used by permission.

# Jesus Is All that I Need!

"Commitment"

As for me and my house,
we will serve the LORD.

(Joshua 24:15)

# "Exactly What I Need"
## Because Jesus Lives...I Can Face Tomorrow

Warm rays of sunshine fell across my shoulder and onto the delicate pages of my open Bible. The light rested on the beautiful message of God's mercy, forgiveness and unending love. The parchment felt warm against my hand as my fingers lovingly traced over the words that promised me hope and eternal life. Messages such as:

> *Show me your ways, O LORD, teach me your paths; guide me in your truth and teach me, for you are God my Savior, and my hope is in you all day long.*
> *(Psalm 25:4-5 NIV)*

> *Blessed are they whose transgressions are forgiven, whose sins are covered. Blessed is the man whose sin the Lord will never count against him.*
> *(Romans 4:7-8 NIV)*

> *If we confess our sins, he is faithful and just and will forgive us our sins and purify us from all unrighteousness. If we claim we have not sinned, we make him out to be a liar and his word has no place in our lives.*
> *(1 John 1:9-10 NIV)*

> *But now he has appeared once for all at the end of the ages to do away with sin by the sacrifice of himself. Just as man is destined to die once, and after that to face judgment, so Christ was sacrificed once to take away the sins of many people; and he will appear a second time, not to bear sin, but to bring salvation to those who are waiting for him.*
> *(Hebrews 9:26-28 NIV)*

I thought to myself, "Lord, thank you. You knew exactly what I needed today." How precious that our beloved Saviour knows just when our tired minds and overwhelmed, distressed hearts need to be comforted and refreshed. He knows better than anyone our great spiritual need and our utter inability to draw, from our own hearts, unending strength to rise above all of life's burdens.

Oh yes, the pages of history are filled with the many who are known and heralded as survivors. These heroes are rightly honoured as noble, well able to struggle and win over unimaginable tortures and rigorous disasters on many levels: physical, mental and social. We have all read of such amazing men and women, but even so, their tremendous drive to win, to live or to survive, is nevertheless still given by Almighty God's great hand of grace and operates within His Sovereign Will and Eternal timetable.

But these same men and women soon find out how completely destitute of strength they are to win at anything in the spiritual realm, because it is a battle and a victory that only God could win on their behalf.

We, in ourselves, are powerless to prevail! And if we are without life in Christ, we are incapable of facing tomorrow triumphantly, either in victory or with eternal purpose or reward. If this is our predicament, we are hopeless and most miserable. But, if we belong to Jesus Christ, then it is a completely different story!

Some still scoff and say that Christ died on the Cross and lays powerless, dead in some cold and forgotten grave. But they know not the Truth of the living Gospel and remain lost in their sins. The Lord Jesus Christ is very much alive and active in the affairs of life today. He is only a prayer away and cares about every detail.

Because *He lives*, you and I *can* face tomorrow! Why? Because Jesus *is* exactly *all* that we need for today, and He is all that we will ever need or want, for all of eternity! How wonderful to know that Jesus is all I need. Indeed, Jesus is exactly what I need.

*"Crises reveal character:  
when we are put to the test  
we reveal exactly the  
hidden resources of our character."*

Author Unknown

"The Lord has placed His treasure of Truth,
not in the golden vase of talent,
but in the earthen vessels of lowly minds."

Charles Haddon Spurgeon
(2 Corinthians 4:7; 1 Corinthians 2:12)

Taken from *Metropolitan Tabernacle Pulpit*, Vol. 35, p. 77.
Used by permission from The Banner of Truth Trust, Carlisle, PA

But because of his great love for us,
God, who is rich in mercy, made us alive
with Christ even when we were dead in transgressions...
For it is by grace you have been saved,
through faith—and this not from yourselves,
it is the gift of God—
not by works, so that no one can boast.

(Ephesians 2:4-9 NIV)

# Precious Heavenly Father,

How grateful I am for Your indescribable Gift of Salvation.
Your unfathomable Love was poured out for me on Calvary's Cross
through the sacrifice of Your only beloved Son, Jesus Christ—Love, of
which I deserve none, dear Lord, but Love with which
You have showered upon me without hesitation!

And dear Lord Jesus, knowing that
"all have sinned and fallen short of the glory of God,"
how do I begin to thank You for Your willingness to
suffer so completely for what should have been my punishment for my sin?
You died in my place when I was still Your enemy so that I could be restored,
eternally forgiven and cleansed from all unrighteousness.
Such Love is too wonderful for me, and beyond all human understanding.

Still, Abba Father, You continually reveal Your great Love to me
through Your dear Son, my wonderful Saviour and coming King,
not only by deigning to live in my heart but also by guiding me every day
through Your Holy Word, by Your indwelling Holy Spirit. Thank You for
bridging the terrible gulf that my sin created, separating me from You.
Lord, thank you that You did not leave me as a prisoner of death's grave
without a living hope or an Eternity without Your Presence and forgiveness.
I am overwhelmed to think that the precious Gift of Salvation, though
offered to all, cost me literally nothing but, in fact, cost you everything!

How simple You have made it for the world to become Your children.
Father, You have told us we cannot earn Salvation ourselves by our own
good works or by simply trying to keep the commandments of the Old
Testament—which is something that is impossible for us to accomplish. Yet,
those laws do indeed reveal our great need of a Saviour. For only You, Jesus,
Who was without sin, could become our Redeemer. Only You could pay the
price for our sins. Only You could wash it all away once and for all.
Only You could truly meet the demand of those laws.

And so, Lord, because of this, I know the joy of being forever safe in
Your gracious Will and plan for my life from day to day, filled with
eternal purpose and peace. I can bask in Your blessed Presence,
hidden in the Secret Place with You, and I know with certainty that I am
one of Your treasured jewels. How amazing to be able to joy in the
"Treasure of Your Company" every moment of every day, and for all
Eternity! Thank You, Lord Jesus, for loving me.

Amen.

# Eager For His Return?

"God's Love"

God has given us eternal life, and
this life is in his Son.

(1 John 5:11 NIV)

## Eager For His Return?

Normally, Willy would be waiting for me by the back door. In fact, you could almost tell the time by his appearances, he was that faithful. And so the first time Willy failed to show up for several days in a row, I imagined that there must be real trouble. Willy's previous visit with me had not been relaxed. He was acting quite strange, not at all like his normal placid cat-self, and that amplified my concern. He had been fidgeting, tense and quite verbal. At one point he suddenly moved off of my lap and ran between the houses; he appeared to be quite ill.

It was now several days without his routine vigil, and I was becoming increasingly concerned. I chided myself later for not making more of an effort to check on Willy's condition that day.

I kept watching the neighbour's house for even a brief glimpse of my little friend, either walking through their kitchen, peeking out of their back door, or better still, standing up on the sill of their upstairs bedroom window.

It was always a humorous sight to see Willy trying to stand sideways, pressed up against the windowpane, while at the same time trying to balance the rest of his body on the very narrow window ledge! It always made me laugh to see him perched up there. Oh, how I longed to have that same reason to laugh again. How he ever managed to get in that position in the first place remains a mystery. If only I could see him one more time, then I could be certain that he was safe and sound.

Over the course of the next few days I caught myself looking out of my kitchen window many times, just hoping and praying that my concerns were unfounded.

However, by the third day I found that I was taking every possible opportunity to check the window again and again. And, I confess, I even created a few new excuses to justify peeking through our kitchen blinds, hoping Willy would be up in the window again.

I remember praying and asking the Lord to grant me this favour concerning little Willy, when all of a sudden God's Word came into my mind and heart in the form of a question. It was as if the Lord questioned me, "Isn't it sad that many believers today do not long or watch for My return with this same eager diligence? Look how eager and intently you are watching for a glimpse of this little animal. Jan, are you still watching for Me in this same way, or have the cares and business of this life smothered and choked out your anticipation for My return? Make sure things and personal hopes never replace your desire to welcome the sight of My coming."

I breathed a prayer of thankfulness for the Lord's gentle rebuke. I set my heart once again to watch with joy and anticipation for the return of my Lord, and a longing to be in His Presence filled my heart. As I thought of my precious Redeemer, the weight of life's demands lifted.

In that same moment, believe it or not, Willy appeared in all his furry glory in the upstairs window! I laughed right out-loud with relief and praise to the Lord for answering my prayers. How glad I was to see that little Willy was safe and sound. How special to know afresh that God cares about every little thing in our lives, including a prayer of concern for a little cat!

The Lord had used a very simple, living illustration to awaken my weary, cluttered heart so that once again I would watch with renewed anticipation for My dear Saviour's soon return.

Now, whenever I see Willy balancing in the window or bounding across the lawn to greet me, I am reminded that one day, very soon, the Lord Jesus Christ will come again to take us to be with Himself in Glory, forever. What a glorious day that will be!

Are you watching and waiting for that Day? Are you longing for Him? If not, perhaps the Lord, in His tender love and great mercy, has a precious "Willy in the window" type of day prepared to encourage your heart also. God's Word is so true,

> *For where your treasure is, there will your heart be also.*
>
> (Matthew 6:21)

# Heaven

Eye hath not seen, nor ear heard,
neither have entered into the heart of man,
the things which God hath prepared for them
that love Him.

(I Corinthians 2:9)

# The Treasure of His Company

"God's Cleansing Power"

Create in me a pure heart, O God...

(Psalm 51:10 NIV)

## Jesus Is The Treasure!

*The treasures we find on this earth*
*Are all but fleeting right from birth.*
*But if we seek the Eternal*
*And trust in His Love supernal,*
*Then we will see with clear measure,*
*Yes, that Jesus is the Treasure!*

# The Treasure of His Company

Here, within the precious *Treasure of His Company*,
I'm shielded by Jesus, and now just content to be
Hidden under His wings; resting in this "Secret Place"—
Basking in His Presence, beholding His blessed face!

His Beauty, His Love, and His great Grace to me unfolds,
While my burdens on His strong arm He still keeps and holds.
Gazing on my Saviour, Master, my Lord and my King—
Songs of worship pour out, and my poor heart leaps to sing!

And daily God's Holy Word reveals just Who He is—
Wonderful, Counsellor—all these names alone are His.
Yes, the Mighty God, and the Everlasting Father,
And the Prince of Peace—indeed, there just is no other.

For certain I know now, I am His and He is mine.
"Lord of lords and King of kings, great Sovereign so Divine,
Create now I pray a cleansed, pure heart, O God in me
That I might not ever harbour one sin against Thee."

Please bring Thyself all Glory as I obey Thy call—
"Dearest Saviour you are my Life, my Joy, and my All;
All my Comfort, all my Strength, and all my good pleasure,
Yes, my precious Lamb of God,
    **You are my true Treasure!**

*For unto us a child is born,
unto us a son is given:
and the government shall be upon his shoulder:
and his name shall be called
Wonderful, Counsellor, The mighty God,
The everlasting Father, The Prince of Peace.*

(Isaiah 9:6)

# Angels With Coloured Strings Attached!
## Revelation 21: 1-27

As I rested on the deck lounge I began to wonder if the grey cloud cover would move on or bring us more rain. A neighbour called out, "It's hard to believe that summer is over and school starts again tomorrow." "Yes, it sure is," I called back. As I thought about it, I looked upwards trying to locate the lone blue jay calling out across the yard and noticed that some of the leaves were already beginning to change. Soon beautiful colours would paint themselves across landscapes and down many old country lanes.

Colour is everywhere, and God uses it liberally on His paintbrush to brighten drab days, just like today. For instance, the sun finally broke through the clouds a moment ago. It lasted just long enough to cause my eyes to focus on the white floral planter here on my back porch. The sunlight lit up a profusion of rich colour before me, and the greyness of the day instantly vanished! All it took was for God to turn on His light.

That light illuminated the sprays of royal blue-purple lobelia tucked in next to the salmon-pink double geraniums. Both the soft and darker tones of greens went well with the white and fuchsia petunias in the background. They were now sitting in God's spotlight. All of this colour was placed against the weathered grey slats of the porch railing. It was a dazzling sight, and it reminded me of my recent Bible readings where the theme of colour seemed to be one of the many points of interest throughout my study.

Throughout the Scriptures we find many references that are painted with expressive words, as if they were actually rich pigment loaded onto God's paintbrush. From the Genesis account of God's covenant promise to never again destroy the world by a flood came the breathtaking colours of the Heavenly Rainbow. A rainbow is a glorious sight when it appears arched across the sky, and it causes every child of God to remember God's great love and mercy and the Gift of Salvation that He alone provides. Every time I see it, I stop to breathe a prayer of praise and thankfulness back to the Lord. I never want to take it for granted. For me, it is always a privilege to witness such a sight. It is like standing on holy ground.

Still other verses tell us that *"though your sins be as scarlet, they shall be as white as snow; though they be red like crimson, they shall be as wool"*. (Isaiah 1:18). We also read of the many detailed portraits of the temple with all of its beauty and royal attire. Wonderful word pictures describe the silver and gold utensils, the ornate wood carvings of the pomegranates and grapes, the candlesticks, the linen robes, the multi-coloured tassels and bells of gold on the hems of the priestly blue robes, the precious stones set into the gold, blue-purple and scarlet ephod that was attached with gold chains to the breastplate—all of it rich with meaning and eternal promise, and of course vibrant with colour (Exodus 28).

When I think of those precious priestly stones, I also think of the New Testament and the book of Revelation. The beauty that details Heaven and its capital city, the New Jerusalem, is indescribable, yet God has left a record with just enough information and colour-filled thumbnail sketches to take our breath away whenever we think about what Heaven will, indeed, be like. We will see all the Promises of God fulfilled, and Eternity will be more than we could ever have imagined it to be.

1 Corinthians 2:9 tells us *"Eye hath not seen, nor ear heard, neither have entered into the heart of man, the things which God hath prepared for them that love Him."* Our hearts cannot help but fill with a longing and a great anticipation to at last be forever with our Lord of Glory. The colours of Heaven are breathtaking, and we will never have to experience another drab day! How could we, when we realize that even the foundation walls of the New Jerusalem are adorned with twelve layers of precious gems? The walls alone are massive in height and measure 200 feet thick! Each layer is made up of a different gem that continually refracts the brilliant, blazing Glory of God! The word descriptions we have give us much to imagine and anticipate.

The first layer of jasper is like that of clear diamonds. The second is made up of brilliant blue sapphires, while the third of chalcedony is a sky blue with coloured stripes. The fourth is a brilliant green emerald, and the fifth is made up of red-and-white striped sardonyx stone. Sardius of various shades of quartz make up the sixth layer. The seventh is chrysolite in transparent gold or yellow hues. Beryl in the eighth layer is of various colours, including shades of green, yellow and blue. The ninth is adorned in topaz, a yellow-green stone. Chrysoprase of gold-tinted green and jacinth in blue or violet in St. John's day, or red and reddish brown zircon of today, make up the tenth and eleventh layers. The crowning layer is purple amethyst, a perfect and beautiful compliment to the streets of gold and the gates of pearl.

Revelation 21:23 tells us there is no need for the sun or the moon, for there is no night in Heaven. The "Lamb is the Light," and His glory illumines the entire Holy City, for the supreme joy of Heaven is the very Person of Almighty God Himself. Indeed every facet mirrors a breathtaking array of beautiful colour as God's Presence and brilliant glory flashes from the New Jerusalem and throughout the re-created universe. Talk about enthusiastic anticipation to behold such beauty: for the beauty that it all reflects is not the inherent beauty or glory of each stone, but the beauty and glory of The Most High God, our precious Lord and Saviour, Jesus Christ!

As I thought about the myriad of angels surrounding God's throne, as well as the angels at each of the twelve gates of pearl, I couldn't help but think of several dear friends in the Lord— Roberta Hooper, Sam Rogers, Bill and Sarah Howlett and Dorothy Wild—all who are, or were, so enthusiastic about the prospect of going to Heaven. Dorothy was filled with great anticipation as she looked forward to the time when we would all be together with the Lord.

After I founded Garments for The Gospel in November of 1996, Dorothy became my first assistant. She helped me to begin building up that ministry. Although Dorothy was suffering serious heart disease, she continually found satisfaction and relief in her cross-stitch work. She did beautiful pieces, and her mark of distinction was her even stitching and her brightly coloured yarns. One piece in particular stands out in my mind.

I vividly recall how excited Dorothy would become every time she would get close to being able to change to a new and vibrant colour. It was the hardest thing for her to restrain from jumping ahead of the pattern and adding a new colour. She used to tell me she could hardly wait to see what the next colour would look like next to all the other colours in the pattern. Nine times out of ten, she would not be able to stifle or resist the urge to introduce the next colour into the mix before she completely finished the colour she was working with! Hers was a contagious enthusiasm for beautiful colour: an enthusiasm that could not be satisfied. It was the same in her anticipation of Heaven.

One day Dorothy showed me the piece she was working on, trying desperately to finish it before her major heart surgery. She was very weak by then, and time was running out. The surgery date was moved up, and all the preparations were in place. The last I heard she was adding more and more colours. Somehow she was able to keep all twenty or more of the long, loose threads on the back tidy and dangling in order. She knew exactly which thread she needed at any given time. The back of her work was never in a tangle, and the threads were never caught in the other stitches—an amazing feat!

Dorothy longed to finish this piece, but the Lord had other plans. You see, Dorothy was working on a beautiful and gloriously coloured angel in flowing garments, designed to look as if they were lit up by the glory of Heaven itself. Her work had carried her into her appointment with Eternity, and Dorothy went into the Presence of her Lord on August 17, 1997. She is safely home. She no longer has to wait to see what God's colours will look like, all stitched together, because she is enjoying every Divine colour He has created. And the angels are perfect, even as Dorothy is now perfect in the Lord, with no dangling coloured strings attached either.

Dorothy's dear sister later finished the piece in her honour. It would be a reminder of a dear lady who loved the Lord with all of her heart and who demonstrated, by her life, a picture of what it means to not only truly anticipate Heaven but to know the joy of being forever with her Lord. Her cross-stitch was only a picture of an angel with coloured strings attached, but now she dwells among them, free of her earthly tent. She is enjoying her precious Saviour and all the indescribable beauty of Heaven, including all of its breathtaking colours. Psalm 91:11-12, NIV, reminds us that *"he [God] will command his angels concerning you to guard you in all your ways; they will lift you up in their hands, so that you will not strike your foot against a stone."* And this verse was true for Dorothy all through her walk with Christ. How wonderful to know that one day, very soon, if we can testify that we truly belong to Jesus, we will also be in the very Presence of our dear Heavenly Father—and like Dorothy, safe in our Eternal Home.

Yes, it is true that we will dwell in the glorious New Jerusalem with its incredible material beauty, but it is also true, however, that nothing will ever compare to the love and mercy of Jesus Christ, or to the awe and wonder of His glorious character or majesty—absolutely nothing! If Christ were not there, then Heaven's glory would be lost. It is Jesus Whom we will worship and adore, not the streets of gold or the precious stones, or even the angels, for they too will bow with us. And so we will know, without a doubt, that Dorothy's angels with the coloured strings attached were, indeed, only a tiny hint of the reality that awaits us in glory. We will worship our beloved Jesus, the worthy Lamb of Glory, and enjoy the *Treasure of His Company* forever! Hallelujah!

*Continue in him, so that when he appears we may be confident and unashamed before him at his coming.*

*How great is the love the Father has lavished on us, that we should be called children of God!*

(1 John 2:28; 3:1 NIV)

## Where Your Treasure Is

He just could not get comfortable. His little body continued to squirm, moving in every direction at first, then forward an inch at a time. He would get up, turn around and try again. This went on for several minutes.

"Young infants," I thought, "squirm and fidget less than this!" And when they do fuss too much, at least mothers go through a checklist looking for discomforts or concerns. If that fails to reveal the problem, these moms have been taught by wise, experienced grandmas to wrap their babies snugly in a blanket and hold them close to the sound of their beating hearts. Once they begin to settle, they speak softly to them with words of love, especially of God's Love, sing Irish lullabies or hum gentle songs and hymns to soothe their restlessness until, at last, they fall asleep.

"How lovely," I thought, but somehow I don't think the neighbours would buy that routine if I applied it to sweet little Willy who, as you know, often visits me, much to my delight!

In many ways Willy is just like a helpless infant, unable to communicate what is bothering him but who does know where he feels safe and secure. Certainly Willy is not a bold or commanding creature. In fact, he is quite timid and quiet in manner. If Willy chases a butterfly, he will just as quickly stop short and run the other way if that butterfly suddenly changes direction and flies toward him. Willy will forfeit the comfort of his own property, allowing big bully cats to sleep all day long on his own porch while he sits and watches from ours. And the most Willy catches on a serious hunt is a few wispy cobwebs and bits of fluff from under the verandah where he finds a cool shelter from the hot sun. He just does not enjoy confrontation. I think his philosophy is live a peaceable life, be generous and share the porch whenever it is absolutely necessary.

Seriously though, as I thought of this young cat, I thought of all infants who are so dependent on their caregivers to do everything for them: training them for every facet of life, nurturing them into maturity to eventually make wise and godly choices for themselves. They need to be taught so many things in the physical, mental, social and spiritual realms. These are precious things: things one cannot teach a cat when it is afraid of the dark.

I comforted myself with the knowledge that Willy might not be able to speak audible words that would bring glory to God or live a life of service to the Lord in the way we trust that our little ones may well do one day, but God teaches us special lessons through His creation. And in turn, we put those lessons into words that can and do bring glory to God. God may use the poetry, devotionals or even these stories of Willy to bless your life as well.

Because of the lessons learned through Willy's gentle spirit, we can go through our own checklists. Like the wisdom of grannies of old, we will find that the Lord will wrap us in His blanket of Love, close to His heart, where we will find rest, refuge and peace.

I began to think about this analogy as Willy finally found his place of rest next to my heart, with my one arm holding him securely. Almost instantly he went to sleep and did not stir a muscle for a long time. At last he was completely content. Even the squirrels failed to awaken him.

The next morning Willy came to visit as usual. He seemed to be back to his normal self and hopped up onto my lap, following his old pattern of pushing along my arm and rolling into a ball. For a few minutes he let me pat his head.

Then it happened. He started to fuss and fidget again. He was very determined to stretch straight out across my lap, pushing with his hind feet, squirming until he had maneuvered himself back up into a semi-sitting position in the centre of my lap, almost facing into my chin! He fell fast asleep. I couldn't believe it. Not only had he completely broken his normal routine, but he was no longer fussing.

"In many ways he really is just like a baby," I thought. The wide brim of my summer hat shaded his head from the sun's heat as I looked down on this trusting animal. The shadow reminded me of Psalm 91 once again and the theme of this book. Verse 1 tells us, "*He who dwells in the shelter* [or the Secret Place] *of the Most High will **rest in the shadow of the Almighty***" (NIV, emphasis added).

The vision of Willy resting in the cast shadow of my hat began to paint a new picture for me, bringing me full circle. I started my journey by accepting God's invitation and receiving His full assurance of Salvation. The joy of my Saviour's presence, whose company I had chosen to call home, became the place of refuge near to the very heart of God, where I could trust Him for everything.

Because I am covered by His wings, I am ultimately shielded from all evil intent and protected from all harm, the exclusive place where Salvation is rock solid and where I have come to "Treasure" His company.

Remember Willy coming timidly to me in the beginning: just his paws on my knee, then half resting on my lap and half resting on the verandah floor, then up on my lap watching for every movement, bird or squirrel? But now Willy pushes along my arm into a ball to his final place near to my heart. As he has come to know and trust my care for him, nothing else satisfies him.

And isn't that the way it is with us in our relationship to our precious Lord and Saviour as infant Christians? We grow more and more to trust Him, until His Presence only is our complete desire. The personal, spiritual relationship we enjoy here on earth in Christ is but a glorious foretaste of Heaven that is offered and promised to each of us. What a treasure that is!

Right now, *"we have this treasure in earthen vessels"* (2 Corinthians 4:7), but one day, very soon, if we belong to the Lord Jesus, we will be forever with the Lord—forever in the Secret Place of the Most High God—for truly *"where your treasure is, there will your heart be also"* (Matthew 6:21, NIV).

Indeed, Jesus is *The Treasure*. He is the One that our hearts should desire—where our hearts needs to dwell.

No wonder we long to dwell
next to His Heart,
for it is only there
that we truly enjoy...

***The Treasure of His Company!***

*I will love thee, O LORD, my strength.*
*The LORD is my rock, and my fortress, and my deliverer;*
*my God, my strength, in whom I will trust; my buckler,*
*and the horn of my salvation, and my high tower.*

(Psalm 18:1,2)

# My Rock and My Salvation

He only is my rock and my salvation;
he is my defence; I shall not be moved.
In God is my salvation and my glory:
the rock of my strength,
and my refuge, is in God.

(Psalm 62:6,7)

The following chorus, "My Rock And My Salvation,"
is based on Psalm 62:6-7. It was composed in the early 1980s
by my husband's dear father,
William G. Howlett, and
was arranged by a long-time family friend,
Mrs. Lynda Wigglesworth-Wray.

Dad went to be with His Lord on August 11th, 1997.

It is our prayer that this chorus will bless
and encourage your heart
and usher in much praise and adoration for our blessed
Redeemer and our Rock, The Lord Jesus Christ.
We would like to share this precious song with you.
May you sing it back to the Lord
as you, too, joy in The Treasure of His Company.

# My Rock and My Salvation

# Together Forever!

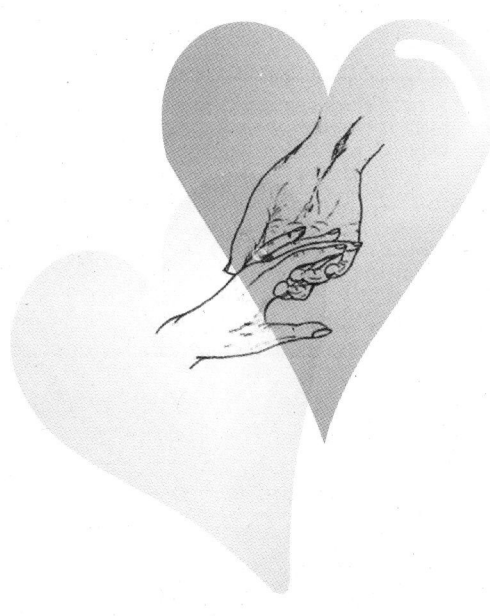

*As for me, I will continue beholding
Your face in righteousness...
I shall be fully satisfied, when I awake
[to find myself] beholding Your form
[and having sweet communion with You].*

(Psalm 17:15 AMP)

# Devotional Notes

# Devotional Notes

# Devotional Notes

# Devotional Notes

# Devotional Notes

# Devotional Notes

# Devotional Notes

# Devotional Notes

# Devotional Notes

# Devotional Notes

# FOLIO ART NOTES
## *All Watercolours by Jan Howlett*

### 1 Mikado Train, "Old 45" #132
"Glorious Journey"
*Verse: "Jesus answered, I am the way, and the truth, and the life."*
*John 14:6 NIV*
*Transparent Watercolour (See Pg. F-97)*
*16" x 20" (41cm x 51cm), 140 lb. Bockingford Cold Press*
*Commisioned: Collection of Allan and Susan Stevens, Scarborough, Ontario.*
*History: The Mikado is a majestic steam engine, 2-8-2 wheel arrangement, built in 1924 by The Baldwin Locomotive Works, and travels a leisurely, maximum speed of 29 miles per hour. It is now a favourite tourist attraction at the California Western Railroad, Fort Bragg.*

### 2 Fishing #Stb-134
"Flying Fish"
*Verse: "I [Jesus] will make you fishers of men..." Mark 1:17 NIV*
*Transparent Watercolour (See Pg. F-97)*
*8" x 2" (20cm x 5cm) 140 lb. Bockingford Cold Press*
*Bookmark Series/Print Collection.*

### 3 Common Gannets # 124
"Commitment"
*Verse: "As for me and my house, we will serve the LORD." Joshua 24:15*
*Transparent Watercolour, (See Pg. F-98)*
*11" x 14" (28cm x 36 cm), 140 lb. Bockingford Cold Press*
*Collection of the artist.*
*One touching trait of the Common Gannet is their ritualistic greeting given to each other. Without fail, no matter how short or long the absence to search for food, it is performed every time one of them returns to the nest. Not only does this display involve sounds, the fencing and clacking of their beaks together, bowing, the raising of their heads, tails and feathers but also preening and the bearing of gifts of seaweed or sticks. Their silhouette when soaring makes an*

*almost perfect cross. They spoke to me of great commitment as well as of God's love and Eternal faithfulness, and therefore, they inspired the artwork of "Commitment."*

## 4 Gryfalcon #119
"Invitation to Worship"
*Verse: "Come, let us bow down in worship, let us kneel before the* LORD *our Maker." Psalm 95:6 NIV*
*Transparent Watercolour (See Pg. F-99)*
*16" x 20" (41cm x 51cm), 140 lb. Bockingford Cold Press*
*Collection of the artist.*

*Adult White Gyrfalcon: In the days when hawking was at its height of popularity in England, the rank of an individual could be easily noted by the particular species of falcon which he carried on his arm: the Gyrfalcon was carried by royalty. These falcons were known for their great courage, swiftness, strength and as a relentless pursuer they commanded the great admiration of men.*

## 5 White Doves #116
"God's Love"
*Verse: "God has given us eternal life, and this life is in his Son [Jesus Christ]..." 1 John 5:11 NIV*
*Watercolour: Transparent and Opaque (See Pg. F-100)*
*16" x 20" (41cm x 51cm), 140 lb. Bockingford Cold Press*
*Commissioned for several private collections in Ontario.*

## 6 Holy Land Lilies #122
"Glorious Resurrection"
*Verse: [God said] "I will never leave thee, nor forsake thee..." Hebrews 13:5*
*Transparent Watercolour (See Pg. F-101 )*
*16" x 20" (41cm x 51cm), 140 lb. Bockingford Cold Press*
*Commissioned for the Collection of Murray and Ruth Ball, Fort Worth, Texas, USA, and also Commissioned by Bill and Linda Tiffin of Tiffin's Creative Centre, Orillia, Ontario, in memory of Cecil and Olive Tiffin, and donated to the Collection of the Doolittle-Carson Funeral Home, Orillia, Ontario.*

*Inspired by the large Arum Lilies growing in the Gardens of Gethsemane, Jerusalem.*

### 7 Christmas Flowers #M009A-C
"Doreen's Amaryllis"
*Verse: "give unto them beauty for ashes..." Isaiah 61:3*
*Jan's Photography Collection with lens effects applied (See Pg. F-101)*
*3" x 2" (8cm x 5cm) Print: 90 lb. Aquarius II Strathmore 500 Ser. Hot press*
*Fridge Magnet Series.*
*Inspired by a lovely Christmas gift received from my very dear friend, Doreen Marley. The glow of evening light led to this photograph idea. I wanted to capture the moment as a lovely reminder of the precious gift of our friendship.*

### 8 Snow Fence #123
"God's Cleansing Power"
*Verse: "Create in me a pure heart, O God..." Psalm 51:10 NIV*
*Transparent Watercolour, (See Pg F-102)*
*16" x 20" (41cm x 51cm), 140 Bockingford Cold Press*
*Commissioned for several private Collections in Ontario.*
*This wintry Beaverton farm scene reveals footprints in the snow. They indicate that an unseen visitor has just passed by and appear to be our invitation to follow them, and complete our journey as well.*

### 9 White N.A. Butterfly #125
"Winged Treasures"
*Verse: "Great is the LORD and most worthy of praise." Psalm 145:3 NIV*
*Transparent Watercolour, (See Pg F-102)*
*8.5" x 11" (22cm x 28cm), 300 lb. D'Arches Cold Press*
*Collection of the artist.*
*Inspired by the North American butterfly.*

### 10 Oro Barn #131
"The Old Road Home"
*Verse: "Thou wilt shew me the path of life..." Psalm 16:11*
*Transparent Watercolour (See Pg. F-103)*
*8.5" x 11" (22cm x 28cm), 300 lb. D'Arches Cold Press*
*Collection of the artist.*
*Inspired by a quaint, old barn in Guthrie, Oro Township, Ontario.*

¹¹ Favourite Forest (God's Presence) # 129
"Precious Fellowship"
*Verse: "How precious...are thy thoughts unto to me, O God!" Psalm 139:17*
*Transparent Watercolour, (See Pg. F-103)*
*16" x 20" (41cm x 51cm), 140 lb. Bockingford Cold Press*
*Collection of Mrs. Frances Spence, Guelph, Ontario.*
*Inspired by unusually shaped trees, bordering a Beaverton Lake Estate, Ontario.*

¹² Apples To Treasure #127
"Apples of Truth"
*Verse: "Keep...my teaching as the apple of your eye..." Proverbs 7:1,2 NASB*
*Transparent Watercolour (Pg. F-104)*
*11" x 14" (28cm x 36cm), 140 lb. Bockingford Cold Press*
*Collection of the artist, & 8.5" x 11" (22cm x 28cm), 140 lb. Bockingford Cold Press*
*Collection of Garfield and Karen Pottle, Orillia, Ontario.*

¹³ Old Oak Tree/Avocet #114
"God's Strength"
*Verse: "Thy God hath sent forth strength for thee..." Psalm 68:28*
*Mixed Media: Transparent Watercolour and Oil Pastel (See Pg. 138)*
*8.5" x 11" (22cm x 28cm), 300 lb. D'Arches Cold Press*
*Private Collections.*

¹⁴ Walls #Gp300
"A Wall With No Door"
*Verse: "You, O LORD, keep my lamp burning...With your help I can advance against a troop; With my God I can scale a wall." Psalm 18: 28a, 29 NIV*
*Transparent Watercolour (See Pg. 140)*
*Corner Artwork for 11" x 14" (28cm x 36cm) matted poem*
*140 lb. Bockingford Cold Press, or Prints on 90 lb. Aquarius II Strathmore 500 Ser. Hot press, Poetry Series.*
*Inspired by an ancient wall with the gate entrance sealed closed, located somewhere in the wilderness, in the Holy Land. It fit the theme of this poem perfectly.*

# BIBLIOGRAPHY

*The Best of C. H. Spurgeon*, Baker Book House, Grand Rapids, MI, ©1979.

Reprinted from *The Best of Tozer*, Compiled by Warren Wiersbe, Christian Publications, Inc., ©1978. Used by permission of Christian Publications, Inc., 800.233.4443, www.christianpublications.com.

*Edges of His Ways*, by Amy Carmichael, The Dohnavur Fellowship, CLC Publications USA, ©1984. Used by permission.

*Flowers Along The Path*, by Esther Carls Dodgen, Barbour Publishing, Inc., Uhrichsville, OH, ©2001. Used by permission.

*Gleanings Among The Sheaves*, by Charles Haddon Spurgeon, Baker Books, ©1977. Used by permission.

*Goforth Of China*, by Rosalind Goforth, ©1937. Public Domain.

*Gold By Moonlight*, by Amy Carmichael, The Dohnavur Fellowship, CLC Publications, USA, ©1935. Used by permission.

*The Greatest Fight in the World*, Pilgrim Publications, Pasadena, TX, ©1990.

*Green Leaf In Drought-Time*, by Isobel Kuhn, Overseas Missionary Fellowship International, ©1988. Used by permission of OMF International.

*The MacArthur New Testament Commentary: Matthew 8-15*, by John MacArthur, Moody Publishers, ©1985. Used by permission.

*The MacArthur New Testament Commentary: Matthew 16-23*, by John MacArthur, Moody Publishers, ©1985. Used by permission.

*Metropolitan Tabernacle Pulpit,* by Charles Haddon Spurgeon, The Banner of Truth Trust, Carlisle, PA., © 1971, Sermon# 1,910;Vol 35. Used by permission.

*The Normal Christian Life,* by Watchman Nee, Victory Press, ©1957. Public Domain.

*Rose From Brier,* by Amy Carmichael, Christian Literature Crusade, ©1933.

*The Treasury of David,* Vol.3, Baker Book House, Grand Rapids, MI, ©1981.

*Worthy Vessels: Clay in the Hands of the Master Potter,* by Nell Kennedy, Zondervan, Grand Rapids, ©1985. Used by permission of Nell Kennedy.

# ABOUT THE AUTHOR AND
# FEEDING HIS LAMBS MINISTRIES

**FEEDING HIS LAMBS MINISTRIES** (FHLM), originally founded in 1977 on a part-time basis, became a full-time ministry in November 1984 as a work of faith, solely dependent upon God's supply through prayer partners and those of like burden. FHLM is not subsidized or underwritten by any organization.

FHLM purposes to come alongside Christian organizations, churches and believers to assist and minister effectively the whole Word of God, to encourage and strengthen the saints and to reach the lost for Christ.

Jan's husband, Ross, is blessed with the wonderful heritage of a godly Christian family dedicated to serving the Lord and a grandfather who was the pastor of the Toronto Sackville Street Mission Church. In later years, Grandpa Howlett became the Visitation Pastor for Calvary Associated Gospel Church on Pape Avenue in Toronto under the late Reverend Stuart Boehmer, senior pastor and former chancellor of Toronto Bible College (TBC), renamed Tyndale University College & Seminary.

Ross was a constable with the Metropolitan Toronto Police Force for fifteen years before resigning to go into full-time faith ministry. He later graduated from Liberty Home Bible Institute.

In response to God's calling upon his life to become an itinerant preacher, Ross fills pulpits of local and surrounding area churches, broadcasts Bible messages over radio and the Internet, conducts in-depth Bible studies and provides counselling.

His work in ministry has included Sunday services, speaking to various church groups ranging from chapel work for boys' camp and challenging today's college and career groups to ministering to seniors, as well as to many police fellowships. He also served as an elder. As a subsidiary role, Ross also ministers musically as a trumpet soloist.

Jan graduated in 1968 with a three-year Missions Diploma from TBC. While in residence she worked among the deaf and hearing children at Reverend Bob Rumball's Church for the Deaf, as well as serving at the Toronto Russian Church, for her Christian service opportunities. After graduation, while awaiting God's final direction for her life, Jan worked as a secretary-receptionist for the Toronto City Hall Health Department.

Ross and Jan were married in August of 1972 and lived in the Toronto area until moving to Orillia in November of 1993. Now as a team, they put a great emphasis on deep Bible study and extensive prayer, dedicating much of each morning to this needed ministry on the behalf of others in need, including organizations and missionaries on the front lines. This entails a great deal of correspondence to encourage and spur them on in their labours.

While Ross and Jan do not have a family of their own, God has privileged them to see many spiritual children born into the Kingdom of God, growing from infancy into mature believers in Christ, firmly grounded in God's Word. Several of these include police officers discipled throughout Ross's police career, and indeed, they remain as special sons to them today, now with families of their own.

**THE SHEPHERD'S GALLERY:** A major portion of Jan's side of this ministry is, as an artist, her Scripture-engraved watercolour pictures and, as an author, her inspirational writings of devotional poetry and meditations. Jan is a self-taught artist, and each painting is the result of her walk with the Lord: not only in joy or heartache, discovering truth or being disciplined by it to trust God in some unexplained dark place, but also as a visible testimony of praise to God's sustaining grace for living the Christian life day by day.

Jan's artwork has been in several local Christian bookstores and art shops, as well as being available at her home office in Orillia, where you will always find the teapot on and a warm welcome awaiting you should you come to visit! From time to time, Jan will also conduct personal art classes in watercolour.

This facet of ministry has once again opened further doors for Jan to speak at ladies' coffee hours and Bible groups, as well as our local Bible conference, sharing devotional and expository style Bible messages. Both Ross and Jan have a deep burden and a heart to share God's Word as opportunities are given and, therefore, fulfill God's mandate to "Feed His Lambs" (John 21:15).

In November 1996, Jan also founded **GARMENTS FOR THE GOSPEL**, (GFTG), a sewing ministry for needy children with the first church-operated chapter beginning at First Baptist Church in Orillia, as well as preparing a fifty-page instructional Starter's Kit for new chapters. Gospel garment labels with "Jesus Loves You, John 3:16," in the child's native language, are sewn right into each item and a gospel tract placed in each pocket whenever possible, literally making them "Garments for the Gospel."

Because of this effort and God's blessing, a number of chapters have sprung up from Fredericton, New Brunswick; Brantford, Ontario, to Alberta, to Texas, to name a few. Several more are seriously praying with the intent of starting their own GFTG in the near future. Many GFTG PJs have been sent, with missionary follow-up, to hundreds of children in Bolivia, Haiti, Latvia, Orillia, Peru, Romania, Uganda, Ukraine, Zambia and, God willing, into the heart of Russia in the near future. In 2002, GFTG added the availability of offering Solo Chapters for those individual ladies not able to connect with a group-operated GFTG but who desire to serve in this ministry on their own, or with the help of one or two helpers. Several have responded enthusiastically since its inception, for which we praise God.

**FEEDING HIS LAMBS RADIO AND INTERNET BROADCASTS** is the newest arm of developing ministry, and operates under the auspices of High Adventure Gospel Communications Ministries Canada, and partners with Bible Voice Broadcasting Network, Leeds, England. Our programming focusses on either fifteen- or thirty-minute expository Bible messages or five-minute "Thought for The Day" programs. They air in various parts of the world, including Africa, Asia, the British Isles, Eastern and Western Europe, India, Ireland and the Marshall Islands. Many listeners are seeking for the answers to life. Those answers can only be found in our Lord Jesus Christ. Still others are hungering for fellowship and encouragement in their Christian walk, while suffering saints need strength and hope. We are privileged to share the Good News, and as our theme song for the Broadcast reminds all of us, the Lord Jesus Christ is a faithful Saviour.

*Great is thy faithfulness (Lamentations 3:23)*

Feeding His Lambs is a full-time faith ministry, solely supported by the free-will offerings, honorariums and love gifts of concerned individuals and those blessed by this ministry. While we do not set specific fees when invitations are extended, we do ask that prayerful consideration be given to meeting travel, ministry and living expenses.

If you wish to support the ongoing ministry needs of our radio broadcasts, please write or e-mail us at the address below or contact High Adventure Gospel Communications Ministries at: **1-800-550-4760**.

If we can be of any further assistance, provide a brochure for any of the branches of ministries cited above, information concerning bookings, the purchase of art work or obtaining further copies of this book, please contact us.

Or, if this book has simply been a blessing in your life, we would love to hear from you. Please contact us by writing,

**FEEDING HIS LAMBS MINISTRIES**
**43 Rosemary Road**
**Orillia, Ontario, Canada L3V 7P9**

*OR* **e-mail us at:**

**hislambs@csolve.net**

**Or visit and listen to the broadcasts at**

**www.biblevoice.org**

*In His Service, until He comes,*
*Ross & Jan Howlett*

Feeding His Lambs:  Word & Music Ministries

## Order Form - BOOKS

To order *The Treasure of His Company,* by Jan Howlett, please use the order form below.

Name: _____

Address: _____

City: _____ State/Prov: _____

Zip/Postal Code: _____ Telephone: _____

E-mail Address: _____

_____ copies @ $24.95 each CDN:    $_____

                   **Sub-Total:**    $_____

**For Books**
**Shipping:** ($4.00 first book + $1.00 each additional book)
                                                   $_____
           **Total amount enclosed:**    $_____

Payable by Cheque or Postal Money Order *Fwd.*

**Send to:**     *Mrs. Jan Howlett*
                     43 Rosemary Road
                     Orillia, ON, Canada L3V 7P9
                     **hislambs@csolve.net**

Please make cheques or money orders payable to Jan Howlett.
Allow time for cheques to clear.

**To Add Poem Prints to Order - see Part B**

*Feeding His Lambs:*  *Word & Music Ministries*

## Order Form - Part B - Poems

To order **Individual decorated Matted Poems with Artwork in 2 corners**, by Jan Howlett, suitable for framing, please use the order form below.

### One Size: 11" x 14" Unframed
### MATT Cols:
### Green #1, Blue #2, Yellow #3, Cream #4, Rust #5

**Print Designs Available:** See pgs. re: Art samples     **Qnty Ea.**

Cover, Pg. 128   A) TTHC Butterfly vignette
                      & Chrysalis                              _____

   Pg. 88      B) Blue Poppy and Buds            _____

   Pg. 104    C) Apples of Truth and Leaves   _____

   Pg. 97      D) Flying Fish & Fish Lure           _____

_____ Copies @ $17.95 each CDN:     $_____

                                 **Sub Total:** $_____

**For Poems**
**Shipping:** ($4.00 first poem + $1.00 each additional poem)

**If Books Ordered ADD Total carried fwd.**     $_____
                    **Total Amount Enclosed:**     $_____

*Please fill in your Order Information*

| [A-D] Print Design | Choice of Poem - give Title | Pg# | Mat Col.# |
|---|---|---|---|
| *Eg: A (TTHC)* | *The Treasure of His Company* | *170* | *1-Green* |
| _____ | _____ | ____ | _____ |
| _____ | _____ | ____ | _____ |
| _____ | _____ | ____ | _____ |
| _____ | _____ | ____ | _____ |

Please make cheques or money orders payable to Jan Howlett.

Allow time for cheques to clear.

Feeding His Lambs:  Word & Music Ministries

## Order Form - BOOKS

To order *The Treasure of His Company*, by
Jan Howlett, please use the order form below.

Name: _____

Address: _____

City: _____ State/Prov: _____

Zip/Postal Code: _____ Telephone: _____

E-mail Address: _____

_____ copies @ $24.95 each CDN:     $_____

                              **Sub-Total:**     $_____

**For Books**
**Shipping:** ($4.00 first book + $1.00 each additional book)
                                                $_____
            **Total amount enclosed:**     $_____

Payable by Cheque or Postal Money Order

**Send to:**     *Mrs. Jan Howlett*     ***Fwd.***
                      43 Rosemary Road
                      Orillia, ON, Canada L3V 7P9

                      **hislambs@csolve.net**

Please make cheques or money orders payable to Jan Howlett.
Allow time for cheques to clear.

**To Add Poem Prints to Order - see Part B**

Feeding His Lambs: *John 21:15* Word & Music Ministries

## Order Form - Part B - Poems

To order **Individual decorated Matted Poems with Artwork in 2 corners**, by Jan Howlett, suitable for framing, please use the order form below.

### One Size: 11" x 14" Unframed
### MATT Cols:
### Green #1, Blue #2, Yellow #3, Cream #4, Rust #5

**Print Designs Available:** See pgs. re: Art samples       **Qnty Ea.**

| | | |
|---|---|---|
| Cover, Pg. 128 | A) TTHC Butterfly vignette & Chrysalis | _____ |
| Pg. 88 | B) Blue Poppy and Buds | _____ |
| Pg. 124 | C) Apples of Truth and Leaves | _____ |
| Pg. 97 | D) Flying Fish & Fish Lure | _____ |

_____ Copies @ $17.95 each CDN:         $_____

                                    **Sub Total:** $_____

**For Poems**
**Shipping:** ($4.00 first poem + $1.00 each additional poem)

**If Books Ordered ADD Total carried fwd.**     $_____
                **Total Amount Enclosed:**     $_____

*Please fill in your Order Information*

| [A-D] Print Design | Choice of Poem - give Title | Pg# | Mat Col.# |
|---|---|---|---|
| *Eg: A (TTHC)* | *The Treasure of His Company* | *170* | *1-Green* |
| _____ | _____ | ___ | _____ |
| _____ | _____ | ___ | _____ |
| _____ | _____ | ___ | _____ |
| _____ | _____ | ___ | _____ |

Please make cheques or money orders payable to Jan Howlett.

Allow time for cheques to clear.